AF583866

Quarterly Essay

Quarterly Essay is published four times a year by Black Inc., an imprint of Schwartz Books Pty Ltd. Publisher: Morry Schwartz.

ISBN 9781760645014 ISSN 1444-884x

Subscriptions – 1 year print & digital (4 issues): $99.99 within Australia incl. GST. Outside Australia $134.99. 1 year digital only: $64.99.

Payment may be made by Mastercard or Visa, or by cheque made out to Schwartz Books. Payment includes postage and handling.

To subscribe, fill out and post the subscription card or form inside this issue, or subscribe online:

quarterlyessay.com
subscribe@quarterlyessay.com
Phone: 61 3 9486 0288

Correspondence should be addressed to:

The Editor, Quarterly Essay
22–24 Northumberland Street
Collingwood VIC 3066 Australia
Phone: 61 3 9486 0288 / Fax: 61 3 9011 6106
Email: quarterlyessay@blackincbooks.com

Editor: Chris Feik. Management: Elisabeth Young. Publicity: Anna Lensky. Design: Guy Mirabella. Associate Editor: Kirstie Innes-Will. Production Coordinator: Marilyn de Castro. Typesetting: Typography Studio.

Printed in Australia by McPherson's Printing Group.

WOODSIDE VS THE PLANET

How a Company Captured a Country

Marian Wilkinson

Australia's huge fossil-fuel exports were always the elephant in the room in the years I reported on climate change and energy matters. Until recently the greenhouse pollution from these exports was seen by most Australian politicians and policy-makers as largely the responsibility of our Asian customers – not ours. That assumption is now unravelling at speed.

Australia's largest gas exporter, Woodside Energy, has become a prime target of the climate movement because it is one of our biggest greenhouse polluters, not only at home but also globally. For over four decades Woodside has worked closely with state and federal governments in Perth and Canberra on the assumption that large amounts of gas would be indispensable to fuel economic prosperity here and in Japan, China and South Korea long into the future. Woodside's interests became enmeshed with the national interest in energy policy, industry policy, trade and foreign policy. Even our spies, at critical points, worked for its benefit. Successive chairs of Woodside had the ear of prime ministers and premiers. Politicians left public life to sit on its board. But when Labor governments locked in behind Woodside's new wave of gas developments, the climate movement drew a line. Their campaign, at times erratic and often rebuffed by Woodside and the politicians, urged Australians to look again at our fossil-fuel exports. The campaign grabbed my interest because it coincided with an upheaval in thinking about climate and energy. The damaging impacts of a warming planet are becoming clearer, and the energy transition is advancing rapidly. Together they pose a growing threat not just to Woodside but to Australia's lucrative fossil-fuel trade.

*

At the top of the long sweeping driveway to Perth's Crown Casino, police vans were lined up outside the entrance leading to the ballroom. Inside, an army of private guards in black suits and white shirts was checking the bags of elderly shareholders arriving for Woodside's annual general meeting. The security was completely over the top and completely understandable. Woodside is under siege from the climate movement. Activists across the nation are outraged by Woodside's plans to power ahead with big new gas projects just as the world is hitting the guardrails of global warming set by the Paris Agreement.

As I made my way to the May 2025 meeting, a small band of protesters stood on a grassy knoll outside the casino grounds, watched over by a squad of motorbike police looking for anyone attempting to breach their containment cordon. The activists held up a large red banner: "Woodside – Fuelling Climate Disaster – Ripping Off Communities – Driving Species Extinction." A towering effigy of the WA premier, "Roger the Cook," arrived wearing a Woodside apron and holding a pan for "Frying the Planet." The WA Greens leader, sporting a sequined Disrupt Burrup Hub t-shirt, mingled with the Drummers for Climate Action.

Climate protesters, Indigenous activists, outspoken academics, green Dockers' fans, worried Nippers' parents, marine scientists, climate scientists, archaeologists, shareholder activists, rebellious artists, famous writers and crusading rock singers – all had waged a determined, relentless, exhausting campaign against Woodside for well over three years. The Perth-based company is castigated by Greenpeace as a "climate wrecker." Its chief executive, Meg O'Neill, is derided as "Methane Meg" by Extinction

Rebellion minstrels. Its benighted chairman, Richard Goyder, along with other Woodside directors, has faced rolling shareholder revolts.

The campaign first took off in late 2021, when activists targeted Woodside's new gas plans for the remote Burrup Peninsula in northwest Australia. That November, O'Neill pressed go on the $16.5-billion Scarborough project – thirteen offshore wells able to produce around 8 million tonnes of liquified natural gas (LNG) a year, processed through the company's expanded Pluto plant on the Burrup. By Woodside's calculations, that's enough fossil fuel to power 8.5 million homes around the world through to 2056.

Scarborough is just one part of Woodside's plans, which include extending the life of the giant North West Shelf (NWS) gas plant, also on the Burrup, until 2070. That plant, which Woodside operates as part of a joint venture with four foreign partners, is the third-largest single industrial emitter of greenhouse gases in Australia. (These emissions do not include those from eventual use of the gas.) To keep the NWS plant running for another forty years, Woodside is proposing to drill some fifty new gas wells over a large area of ocean off Broome in the Browse Basin, a reserve it calls "Australia's largest untapped conventional gas resource." Environmentalists are alarmed because the basin is home to Scott Reef, one of Australia's most diverse coral ecosystems. Greenpeace chief executive David Ritter denounced Woodside's plans as monstrous, "the worst climate-polluting infrastructure proposed anywhere in the nation." The Australian Conservation Foundation's chief executive, Kelly O'Shanassy, was equally appalled, labelling the Burrup Hub plans "the Southern Hemisphere's largest gas carbon bomb."

Calculating all the greenhouse gas emissions from Woodside Burrup Hub plants, including those released by its overseas customers, is a difficult exercise. Climate scientist Dr Bill Hare and his team at the think-tank Climate Analytics have estimated that from 2026 to 2070 these emissions could amount to 6 billion tonnes. This, they said, would be 25 per cent more emissions than all of Australia is expected to release while getting to net zero by 2050. Woodside's response to the "carbon bomb" claims is that both the company and its customers have climate plans to get to net-zero emissions and these need to be taken into account. But Woodside's own climate plan has drawn intense criticism because its net-zero target is "aspirational" and it has no real way to account for its customers' emissions.

The company's recent annual general meetings have become fraught affairs as opponents of Woodside's climate plan seek to get their voices heard. In 2023 activists from Disrupt Burrup Hub attempted to force evacuation of Woodside's AGM by simulating a gas leak with a stink bomb. Western Australia's state security investigation group, part of its counter-terrorism response team, intercepted one of the activists as he tried to enter the meeting and foiled the plot. Three activists involved were charged with aggravated burglary with intent – charges that were later downgraded. But the bigger threat to the company that year came from inside the AGM and was less easily quashed.

One of Woodside's high-profile directors, the former Howard government resources minister Ian Macfarlane, saw more than a third of shareholders vote against his re-election, many of whom were worried about Woodside's plan to deal with climate change. Two fellow directors up for re-election also took a hit. While all ultimately survived the revolt, several big investors supported a call by a shareholder activist group, the Australasian Centre for Corporate Responsibility, to hold the directors accountable for what it called Woodside's ineffective climate plan.

The vote against Macfarlane looked like a pivotal moment for Australia's climate movement and pointed to serious trouble ahead for Woodside. Shareholder activists believed their message was finally being heard: Woodside's fossil-fuel growth strategy could be bad for investors. Alex Hillman, a former climate change adviser with Woodside who left and joined ACCR, gave the company a prescient warning: "Climate risk matters and if shareholder concerns are blatantly ignored, director votes won't breeze through an AGM." He urged Woodside's Goyder to reflect on the result.

Sure enough, in the lead-up to Woodside's 2024 AGM, Goyder faced a shareholder push against his chairmanship. Some of Australian's biggest superannuation funds, including HESTA (for health workers) and AustralianSuper, cited "ongoing concerns" about Woodside's plan to get to net-zero emissions by 2050. By then, the super funds were being pummelled by the big environment groups, which ran full-page ads calling on them to vote down the climate plan. Goyder survived as chair, but three major Australian super funds, along with Australia's Future Fund, Norway's largest private pension fund, Britain's largest asset manager and several US pension funds – some 58 per cent of voting shareholders – opposed Woodside's Climate Transition Action Plan. It was the world's first majority vote against a public company's climate plan.

But then, in November 2024, Donald Trump was elected as US president. Immediately he pulled America out of the Paris Agreement. His "drill, baby, drill" mantra and crusade against renewables led to a new mood of optimism in the global fossil-fuel industry.

As Woodside's shareholders waited to enter the 2025 AGM, I could sense both nervous tension and a palpable confidence among the directors. Over morning tea, Ian Macfarlane chatted cheerfully with the three directors up for re-election, including Ben Wyatt, Western Australia's former Labor treasurer, and Ann Pickard, a veteran oil and gas executive who worked for Mobil and Shell before joining Woodside, where she chairs the board's sustainability committee, overseeing the fraught climate plan. Goyder had no doubt all would survive this year's shareholder vote.

When he and O'Neill took their seats on the ballroom stage, giant screens lit up behind them with images of Woodside's gas projects. The directors sat on the main floor; so too did twenty or more climate protesters who had slipped into the meeting undetected. Goyder welcomed everyone with a nod to the new world order under Trump – roiling share markets, trade wars and American climate ambition in retreat. "Our climate strategy is well suited for current political and market realities, which indicates the energy transition is likely to unfold in a way that is not linear or uniform across the globe," he told them with silken understatement before handing over to his CEO.

When Meg O'Neill took the podium, she told the shareholders in her calm monotone that they could have "confidence in Woodside's considered, disciplined strategy to thrive through the energy transition." But less than a minute into her speech, a deafening, high-pitched whistle pierced the room, sending the black-suited security guards scurrying to find the culprit. As O'Neill tried to soldier on over the racket, a Woodside tech hit the play button for the giant screen and a voiceover boomed across the room: "Gas, like the natural gas produced by Australia's Woodside, helps meets one of the great challenges of the world ..."

O'Neill warned the activists that she would not tolerate disruption – "we've got plenty of those videos." But the activists had plenty of those whistles. The seventh whistle-blower I saw jump up was Greenpeace activist turned Greens politician Sophie McNeill, who kept blowing until she was hustled out the door. By the time the twelfth activist let fly, tempers were fraying. "Take the fucking whistle off him, for God's sake," the shareholder in front of me yelled.

By the time Meg O'Neill finished her speech, the activists were already heading back to the grassy knoll to shoot their Instagram posts. "We blew the whistle on Woodside this morning," Sophie McNeill told her followers. "Meg O'Neill is a climate criminal."

More important than the activists' hijinks that day were the critical votes for the directors. The results signalled that while shareholder dissent on Woodside's climate plan was more muted, it had not been silenced. The climate plan wasn't put up this year, but that meant the vote on director Ann Pickard, chair of the sustainability committee, became a lightning rod for frustrated shareholders. Almost 20 per cent of them voted against Pickard. Among the big Australian superfunds, HESTA voted against her, but Australia's biggest, my fund AustralianSuper, backed Pickard and the other directors. A leading shareholder in Woodside, AustralianSuper has many blue-collar members from the Australian Workers' Union (AWU). The vote demonstrated faith in the board and its gas growth strategy.

At the AGM, shareholder activist Alex Hillman questioned Goyder about whether Woodside's new fossil-fuel investments would do anything to improve shareholder returns. "Woodside has significantly and chronically underperformed its peers while persisting with a high-cost, high-risk, fossil-fuel growth strategy," he argued.

Goyder admitted, "Our share price performance hasn't been as we would like," but brushed off concerns: "Our business is going well …"

O'Neill is unabashed about Woodside's go-for-growth gas strategy. It mirrors that of her peers in top oil and gas companies around the world – ExxonMobil, Shell and Chevron. Her game plan is their game plan. Strive to thrive through the energy transition. The war in Ukraine reinforced that strategy by putting the world on edge over energy security and affordability. It was great news for gas and bad news for the climate.

While the gas companies say they still support the Paris Agreement, few are willing to shrink their own fossil-fuel business. Dr Bill Hare, who crunches the numbers on pathways to net zero, said the companies' claims do not add up. "If you look at Woodside, Shell, BP, they're all aligned around a 2.5°C warming pathway," he said. "We already know that 2.5 to 3°C warming is going to be catastrophic and wildly inconsistent with the Paris Agreement."

When I caught up with Meg O'Neill soon after the AGM, she was keen to talk about the campaign against the company and challenge the criticism of climate scientists such as Hare. "I think it's a pretty long bow to draw to look at one reasonably small energy producer's outlook and conclude a temperature rise from it." She pointed out that the Intergovernmental Panel on Climate Change has different modelling scenarios on pathways to net zero. "I don't think any of us at Woodside would try to be so clever as to pick exactly where the world is headed and how it's going to get there." But several of O'Neill's peers are already saying publicly that the world is unlikely to make net-zero emissions by 2050. Among them is her old boss at ExxonMobil, chair and CEO Darren Woods, who argues that consumers won't pay the price needed for a clean energy transition. He bluntly told *Fortune* in 2024: "what's being done today, the infrastructure investments that are being made, we're not on the path to 2050. I think most objective analysis would tell you that."

O'Neill wouldn't comment directly on Wood's pessimistic scenario, but she didn't dismiss it either. "I think the world is starting to realise that decarbonisation is complex and there are nations in the world who are prioritising economic development over decarbonisation. So, will the world get there? I think that's a decision for the United Nations to help facilitate."

The campaign against Woodside is testing the limits of climate activism in Australia. It's also testing the gas industry's promise to shareholders that it can maintain long-term profits by investing in new fossil-fuel projects as it looks increasingly likely the world will cross the threshold of 1.5°C of global warming. Many of the battle-hardened activists know their campaign will likely not stop Woodside's projects going ahead. Instead, they believe the protests, the direct action, the legal challenges and the lobbying will impose a social and financial cost on Woodside.

For Piers Verstegen, who led the Conservation Council of Western Australia for over twelve years, the fight against Woodside is a moral imperative. "If you look around the world everywhere, there's community groups and scientists and others that are trying their darndest in whatever ways they can muster to stop fossil fuels being extracted out of the ground. If we just ignore that responsibility here in Western Australia, then we're not playing our role."

For Australia's political leaders, the climate campaigners' demand that Woodside should give up its "carbon bomb" projects and allow its business to shrink rather than grow is akin to economic vandalism. Woodside and its NWS project are synonymous with the bold frontier resource development that created Australia's prosperity. O'Neill and the Woodside board are confident their political support will survive a campaign over climate change.

Woodside argues the world needs its new gas projects to "keep the lights on" during the energy transition as the world aims to reach net-zero emissions by 2050. O'Neill hammers this case: that her company has a vital role to play in helping the world decarbonise by moving from coal to gas. Since the Paris Agreement, this has been the agreed narrative between big gas companies and the nation's major political parties. But as natural disasters fuelled by climate change escalate and global emissions keep rising, this narrative is being upended.

MEG FROM EXXON

Meg O'Neill is steeped in the culture of the big American oil and gas companies, like many of the men who ran Woodside before her. She does not have the bluster and ego of some in the business, but her frank, no-nonsense manner underscores her can-do approach. She grew up in the Rocky Mountains state of Colorado and joined the oil giant Exxon straight after graduating from the Massachusetts Institute of Technology, where she studied chemical and ocean engineering. She spent almost a quarter of a century with ExxonMobil before jumping to Woodside. Her Perth nemesis, billionaire Andrew "Twiggy" Forrest, once described O'Neill as "hard-edge trained by the biggest liar we've ever seen around climate change over the last forty years, and that's ExxonMobil." But it was O'Neill's Exxon training that put her in line for the top job at Woodside. She is a very effective business executive, according to former Woodside staff. "She's across the detail. She can get stuff happening and is really good at working through a to-do list," said Alex Hillman.

O'Neill earnt a reputation early in her career for confronting challenges head-on. Her first Australian boss, Peter Coleman, spotted her talent when Exxon sent her to Indonesia two decades ago. "I was chairman of Indonesia for Exxon," Coleman recalled, "Meg was running the engineering team. We promoted her to head up our operations up in Aceh." At the time, Exxon's lucrative gas operation in Aceh had only recently seen off a threat from rebel Muslim separatists who had shut down the plant. The Indonesian military, who were waging a brutal war against the rebels, were put on the company payroll to protect Exxon's gasfields. O'Neill arrived in Aceh right after the devastating 2004 tsunami that ended the rebellion. She was an outspoken, young, white, gay American woman who managed to run the giant Aceh gas operation successfully for several tough years.

But it was O'Neill's stint at ExxonMobil's head office in Houston, Texas, that likely helped steel her for the opposition she faces today. She was appointed executive adviser to Exxon's legendary chairman and CEO Rex

Tillerson in 2016, just after the Paris Agreement was signed. President Barack Obama was still in the White House and Exxon was being roiled by its first big shareholder revolt over climate change.

That revolt was fuelled by an exposé published in *The Los Angeles Times* and *Inside Climate News* accusing Exxon of burying its own scientific research, dating back to the 1970s, on the dangers of global warming caused by burning fossil fuels. Exxon denied a cover-up, but Tillerson's predecessor had notoriously run a decades-long campaign funding climate science sceptics to spread doubt about the link between fossil fuels and global warming. The exposé became part of the #ExxonKnew campaign embraced by activists. More damaging to Exxon, the exposé was also cited in a string of lawsuits that accused the company of withholding information on global warming from the public and shareholders. (None of the lawsuits to date has been successful.)

When O'Neill arrived at Houston headquarters, the shareholder revolt led by the Church of England trust and the New York State Comptroller was big news. At the AGM that year, O'Neill's boss confronted shareholder activists with some of the same arguments O'Neill uses today: we need more new investment in gas for energy reliability. "The world is going to have to continue using fossils fuels, whether they like it or not," Tillerson said, predicting oil and gas would still provide 60 per cent of the world's energy by 2040.

That early ExxonMobil shareholder revolt was defeated. In November that year, Donald Trump was elected president for the first time. He pulled America out of the Paris Agreement and named Tillerson as his secretary of state. O'Neill stayed on in Houston briefly to work for his successor, Darren Woods, who is still ExxonMobil's CEO. She and Woods went to the World Petroleum Congress in Istanbul in the summer of 2017, where the world's big oil and gas companies were thrashing out their response to Paris. Woods publicly supported the Paris Agreement and urged Trump to stick with it. The industry was promoting gas as the vital "transition fuel" needed to get the world to net zero. There was a killing to be made as Europe and Asia moved away from more emissions-intensive coal-fired power.

At that Istanbul conference, O'Neill ran into her old colleague Peter Coleman, who was now chief executive of Woodside in Australia. They had dinner and he offered her a senior executive job. When O'Neill landed in Perth a year later, Woodside was at a crossroads. Its rich reserves in the NWS gasfields were declining and to keep growing Woodside desperately wanted a big new gas project. Coleman's best hope was the Scarborough gasfield 375 kilometres off the Burrup Peninsula. He had just done a US$744-million deal with Exxon that included buying its stake in Scarborough. Woodside now controlled 75 per cent of the Scarborough field.

Fortune favours the brave, and it did for O'Neill. Woodside's remaining 25 per cent partner in Scarborough was the Big Australian, BHP, but its directors had been stalling on the project for years as gas prices stayed weak and COVID-19 smashed the energy market. Coleman abruptly quit as CEO of Woodside in April 2021, but just months later, in a seismic decision, BHP announced it would hive off its entire emissions-heavy oil and gas business, including Scarborough, to Woodside in a multi-billion-dollar share merger deal. The deal gave Woodside all BHP's oil and gas assets, including its stakes in Scarborough, the Browse Basin and the North West Shelf.

The day the deal was formally announced, Goyder and the board anointed Meg O'Neill as Woodside's new chief executive. She was now head of Australia's largest oil and gas company, the largest energy company listed on the ASX, and a global top-ten exporter of LNG. The new business stretched from Bass Strait to the Gulf of Mexico. At her first press conference as chief executive, O'Neill committed to reduce Woodside's greenhouse gas emissions by 15 per cent by 2025 and by 30 per cent by 2030, and to get to net zero by 2050. "All of our investment decisions will be made through the lens of the energy transition," she promised. But at the same time, she flagged she wanted the giant Scarborough gas project to go ahead. It was, she said, "the most significant growth opportunity in the portfolio."

Woodside green-lit Scarborough three months later. The "carbon bomb" was dropped and "Methane Meg" was born. In unfortunate timing, O'Neill's announcement came just over a week after the new global Climate Pact was agreed in Glasgow, aiming to keep the Paris Agreement on track and the goal of 1.5 alive. Climate activists vented their fury online. "Before the ink is dry on the Glasgow Climate Pact, Woodside has hit the accelerator on the single largest new fossil-fuel project in Australia in recent memory," wrote ACCR's Dan Gocher.

O'Neill would stare down the climate movement for the next four years with the same determined efficiency that she brought to pulling off Woodside's multi-billion-dollar gas plans.

In Australia's corridors of power, the Scarborough announcement was met with wild enthusiasm. The prime minister, Scott Morrison, said he "did a bit of a jig" outside the parliamentary chamber when he heard the news. "I couldn't be more thrilled," he told the Business Council. "That's such a shot in the arm for our economy." Western Australia's Labor premier Mark McGowan hailed it as a "boon" for jobs and development in the west – an echo of the enthusiasm that greeted Woodside's arrival on the Burrup Peninsula over four decades ago.

A GAS EMPIRE RISES

After a short drive from the port of Dampier, on Australia's remote northwest coast, you hit a road that cuts across the Burrup Peninsula and brings you to an often-deserted visitor centre perched on the top of a hill. From here you get a spectacular panoramic view of the Karratha gas plant, spread over two square kilometres, bounded by the blue waters of Withnell Bay below and the red rock hills of Murujuga National Park behind you. The first time I saw the plant I was stunned; no image quite captures its breathtaking size and scale. I realised why it's celebrated as one of the greatest engineering feats in Australian history – and why most of us, especially on the east coast, have no real idea of what it is or does. The visitor centre, even when it's open, doesn't offer tours of the plant: it's strictly off-limits to the public.

The Karratha plant is the heart of the NWS project. This was Australia's first LNG export plant. When construction began in the 1980s, it was the biggest engineering project being built in the oil and gas industry anywhere in the world.

There are five LNG "trains" at the plant; these are basically giant refrigerators that treat and freeze the gas to a temperature of –161°C, reducing it to a liquid 1/600th of its original size so it can be shipped to Japan, South Korea and China. Each train is several hundred metres long. Together they can produce 16.9 million tonnes of LNG a year for export – although one train is offline. Two separate domestic "trains" process gas for the Dampier-to-Bunbury pipeline, to power homes and industries throughout Western Australia, including Perth, over 1500 kilometres to the south.

The Karratha plant is connected to huge offshore gas platforms by two trunklines that run underwater 135 kilometres out to sea. The platforms, crewed by workers, are anchored to the seabed and built to withstand the wild cyclonic weather and powerful waves that can buffet this region. Here lie the gasfields of the North West Shelf, the famous gas-rich area of the continental shelf off the West Australian coast. The gas is buried in reservoirs deep below the seabed. The whole project is largely powered by gas. While Woodside is the operator of the plant, at the entrance to the visitor centre you see the proud logos of the joint venture partners whose money and expertise helped make the NWS project happen – Australia's BHP, UK oil majors Shell and BP, US oil giant Chevron, and the mighty Japanese conglomerates Mitsubishi and Mitsui (MIMI). China's National Offshore Oil Company (CNOOC) took up its interest in 2004, when exports to China began.

These days, BHP's share has been merged into Woodside's and Chevron is also getting out, meaning Woodside will soon own half the $34-billion project. This holds big risks for the company. The lucrative gasfields linked to the NWS project are depleting, but Woodside wants to keep this huge plant operating and profitable. It is hoovering up gas from other fields, both offshore and onshore, to fill the trains so it can keep selling to its customers for decades to come. Without new gas, Woodside would eventually have a gargantuan stranded asset on its books, which would cost untold millions to decommission.

This helps explains why Woodside and O'Neill celebrated when the WA state government approved the NWS extension project last December to keep the plant operating until 2070. It also helps explains why O'Neill lobbied so loudly for the Albanese government to approve the extension as well, which it did after the May 2025 federal election. And it explains why Woodside wants both governments to approve its drilling of new offshore wells in the Browse Basin, even though it will need to build a 900-kilometre undersea pipeline to feed the gas back to the plant. It will also need to deal with the high CO_2 content in the gas reservoir by injecting some of it into rock formations beneath the sea in an expensive carbon capture and storage operation.

Looking down at the vastness of the Karratha plant, you realise why Woodside's LNG business is so dependent on government support. This plant could never have been built without it. And today, as we count the cost of every tonne of greenhouse gas emissions, this plant can only keep operating if both state and federal governments are willing to accept that Woodside's gas plans are not a threat to Australia's commitment to the

Paris Agreement. One of the difficult questions being asked by the climate movement is whether a state government so deeply committed to the gas industry here for well over forty years, under both Labor and the Coalition, can make that judgement impartially.

Western Australia's former Labor premier Carmen Lawrence is one who doubts the state government can do this. She believes the gas industry "has got away with murder" and politicians in both major parties won't question it on climate change. "I've been deeply disappointed by the attitude of successive Labor governments to climate change policy generally, but particularly to the blind spot of the impact of burning fossil fuels," she told me. "The idea is that West Australians think this is a mining state and anything that undermines that comfortable perception is likely to be politically unpalatable. People will mark you down if you are seen in any way to constrain or criticise it."

Political support for the gas industry is deep and bipartisan here. At the University of Western Australia's business school, one of the state's longest serving premiers, Colin Barnett, has been busy writing speeches pushing gas development since he was swept from office by Labor in 2017. The Liberal stalwart thinks the activists' campaign will have little to no impact. "Western Australia is conscious of environment and climate change and all that, but Western Australia is very much a mining state. You won't find a family in Western Australia that hasn't got a relative that somehow works in the mining industry," he told me. "It's arguably the world's biggest mining and petroleum economy anywhere. We rival, probably, Texas – the heydays of Texas."

Barnett spent almost three decades in state politics, for over half that time running the state's energy and resources policy, first as minister then as premier. During his parliamentary career, the LNG industry quadrupled in size and the state's greenhouse gas emissions rose. As Barnett sees it, Woodside pioneered an extraordinary gas boom that enriches the state and employs its people, and he can't imagine why this should change. But Barnett knows better than most that the success of Woodside and the gas industry in the west rests heavily on government support.

Three contentious issues challenged that support: climate change, Indigenous heritage and, of course, money – taxes and royalties. The early history of Woodside sheds a lot of light on how both the WA government and the federal government heavily supported Woodside, baking the North West Shelf into the collective political psyche and fostering the assumption that what's good for Woodside is good for the state.

*

Woodside was the 1960s dream of a blueblood Melbourne stockbroker, Geoff Donaldson, and a wily accountant, Rees Withers, whose small Victorian gas company was going broke. Their luck changed dramatically when they hired a brilliant geologist, Nicholas Boutakoff, the immigrant son of Russian aristocrats. He persuaded them to buy an exploration permit larger than the British Isles over the North West Shelf. The permit cost them just £100 and a promise to put up funds for exploration. With this was born the greatest commercial venture of the time in Australia. To fund exploration costs, the Woodside men hawked their permit around some of the biggest oil and gas companies in the world. Eventually, a new Woodside Petroleum Company was formed in 1976. Shell, BHP, BP and Chevron became joint venture partners, with Woodside as project operator. To keep a seat at the table, Woodside had to raise an eye-watering amount of money. The WA Liberal premier, Sir Charles Court, was eager to help, seeing a bonanza of jobs, development and revenue for the state.

The gas on the North West Shelf is owned by the Commonwealth because it lies in Australia's offshore economic zone, beyond the state coastal limits. A royalty arrangement between Canberra and the states was agreed in 1979 which gave Western Australia around two-thirds of the NWS take. As part of this deal, the NWS project would advance in two stages, starting with a domestic gas plant supported by the WA government. The idea was that this revenue would help Woodside and partners fund the second stage, the huge, lucrative LNG export plant.

"The state government basically underwrote the project through its utility, the State Energy Commission," Barnett explained. Under an onerous contract the SEC signed with Woodside and the joint venture partners, the state funded the $1.1-billion Dampier-to-Bunbury pipeline so the SEC could sell the gas to power homes, businesses and a burgeoning minerals-processing industry. But the contract had a brutal "take or pay" clause forcing the SEC to pay for *all* the domestic gas supply from the NWS project. It was Woodside's way of getting a guaranteed cashflow to service its bank loans.

The contract pushed the SEC to the brink of bankruptcy, because it signed up for far more gas than it could sell. By early 1985 it was clear the government utility could default. The new Labor government in Perth, led by Brian Burke, demanded Woodside renegotiate the contract. Woodside's bankers went into a spin, refusing to roll over $2 billion in loans. The whole NWS project and the dream of gas-powered development suddenly faced financial collapse. So Woodside and its partners turned for help to the Hawke Labor government in Canberra and its resources minister, Gareth Evans. Canberra found it had little choice but to increase its financial support for the project.

In his memoir, Evans gives an extraordinary account of being confronted with the "North West Shelf bombshell," as he called it. "It was a very, very big deal," Evans told me. "It was Australia's biggest resources project at the time and one on which much of the future of the economy was riding." By this he means the future of the LNG industry and of gas power for the lucrative WA minerals industry. After a round of dramatic meetings with the prime minister, the treasurer and the heads of Woodside, Shell and BHP, all parties agreed to a solution based on what Evans called the "equality of pain" principle. The federal government gave up its royalties on the domestic gas from the North West Shelf for twenty years, while the state government agreed to use part of its share of royalties to prop up the SEC.

This was just the beginning. The WA Treasury later calculated that by 2010 its total support for the NWS project had exceeded $8 billion.

The crisis tightly bound both state and federal governments to the NWS project, but by then foreign control over it had increased. Woodside had sold down some of its stake to the Japanese companies Mitsubishi and Mitsui (MIMI), which were keen to get involved given the project's long-term sales contracts with Japanese buyers. In the end, Woodside was still the project operator, but foreign interests had the lion's share of the nation's biggest export gas project, and Japan's leading companies had a big voice in the Australian gas industry, one they use loudly today.

Royalties from the NWS project did eventually flow, but they were not the bonanza once imagined. Australia did not follow Norway's path and tax the oil and gas industry heavily or put the revenue into a sovereign wealth fund for the national benefit. According to Woodside, over the last four decades, the NWS project has paid more than $40 billion in combined federal royalties and excise – but that amounts to only around $1 billion a year. Because of its royalty regime, the NWS project was exempted from Australia's so-called "super profits tax," the petroleum resource rent tax (PRRT), when it was first introduced by the Hawke government. Even when this exemption was lifted, the most recent federal treasury analysis predicts that the NWS project is unlikely ever to pay PRRT.

When the Hawke government ditched federal royalties on new gas projects and replaced them with the PRRT, it never really worked for LNG projects, because the companies could write off their huge capital costs on infrastructure against their profits. Chevron's Gorgon and Wheatstone projects, Shell's Prelude floating LNG project, the Japanese Inpex-led Ichthys project and Woodside's second LNG project, Pluto, pay no royalties for the gas they extract from Commonwealth gasfields off Western Australia, and until recently paid no PRRT super profits tax.

"The PRRT was specifically designed during the Hawke years for quick profit oil projects with less intensive infrastructure compared to a gas project," researcher Dr Diane Kraal explains. "By contrast, today we're collecting meagre PRRT on gas due to its costly infrastructure. That's why the gas companies love the PRRT, because they know they've done their sums, they've got their spreadsheets, they know they're paying a lot less tax under the PRRT as compared to the old royalty system." A Monash University academic, Kraal has spent decades researching oil and gas tax revenues in Australia. Her work is backed up by the 2023–24 federal budget papers, which found that "not a single LNG project has paid any PRRT and many are not expected to pay significant amounts of PRRT until the 2030s." This is despite LNG being Australia's third-largest export after iron ore and coal in 2023–24, with export revenue at around $70 billion.

When the climate battle over Woodside's gas expansion escalated, leading campaigners joined forces with federal crossbench politicians and the Australia Institute think-tank to hammer the argument that the LNG export industry was screwing taxpayers and domestic gas users. Independent ACT Senator David Pocock slammed the loss of royalties and the lack of PRRT payments as "daylight robbery" by "absolute leeches" in the gas industry. He also blasted the industry's slim company tax payments over years as "scandalous." The attacks incensed WA politicians and the gas industry but put pressure on the Albanese government, which in 2024 passed a modest reform to the PRRT with the support of the Greens. It tightened up some loopholes and has seen the big LNG projects in the west (but not the North West Shelf) finally expected to pay some PRRT.

More importantly, a crackdown on the gas industry by the Australian Tax Office over capital cost deductions also had a big impact on the foreign gas giants' company tax payments. This, along with a boost in profits after the Ukraine war and Woodside's merger with BHP, saw Chevron, Shell and Woodside make it onto Australia's top twenty corporate taxpayers list in 2022/23. But Kraal, for one, is not satisfied. She wants royalties on Commonwealth gas to be restored. "I mean, these resources are owned by the people of Australia and it's the Commonwealth that manages it," Kraal explained. "And so we owners of this resource expect some sort of return."

Piers Verstegen, once a senior adviser to the WA government and now a veteran climate campaigner, recognises that the domestic gas made possible by the NWS project and others that followed has been beneficial to Western Australia. But he wants to convince the politicians that those times are coming to an end and they need to look to the net-zero future, when gas use will shrink as it is increasingly replaced by renewables. "If you put the royalties part of it aside, if you put the taxes part of it aside, which we've never done well on at all, the LNG industry has given us domestic gas, cheap domestic gas. And it has enabled a whole lot of industries to occur and Western Australia has benefited from that. There's no doubt about that," he acknowledges. "But I think that era is over. And if you just try to drive forward by looking in the rearview mirror all the time, you're probably going to crash."

*

So what does the future hold for the North West Shelf? Woodside and the gas industry have been aware for years – since the very beginning of the NWS project – that the greenhouse gas emissions released from burning their product would need to be reduced or the industry – not to speak of the planet – could eventually face an existential crisis.

In 1988 a confidential document was circulated at the Dutch headquarters of Shell, Woodside's partner. It was titled "The Greenhouse Effect" and it opened with the line, "Man-made carbon dioxide, released into and accumulated into the atmosphere, is believed to warm the earth through the so-called greenhouse effect." It explained this was mainly due to fossil-fuel burning and deforestation. While the paper noted that modelling the consequences involved some uncertainty, it warned the greenhouse effect "may amplify the warming by predicted factors ranging from 1.5° and 3.5°C." If this happened, the paper explained, there could be changes in sea level rise, rainfall and weather. "These changes could be larger than any that have occurred over the last 12,000 years. Such relatively fast and dramatic changes would impact on the human environment, future living standards and food supplies, and could have major social, economic and political consequences."

That same year, Woodside's board and the rest of the oil and gas industry heard these warnings go public around the world. NASA climate scientist Dr James Hansen made a dramatic appearance before the US Senate, declaring that global warming was happening and was caused by burning fossil fuels. In November that year, the United Nations set up the Intergovernmental Panel on Climate Change.

For the next quarter of a century Woodside and its partners made minimal efforts to confront their emissions problem and Woodside's senior leadership often pushed back against federal climate legislation. That was until the Paris Agreement in 2015, when suddenly global gas executives were welcoming the climate scientists' ambition to limit global warning below 2°C and as close to 1.5°C as possible.

The reason for the volte-face was clear in the lead-up to the UN climate conference in Paris. In June 2015, the chief executives of Europe's biggest gas companies, including Shell and BP, wrote an open letter to the *Financial Times* calling on the world to recognise "the major role natural gas can play in addressing climate change." They argued, "The case is simple," because burning gas generated half the carbon emissions of coal. At the World Gas Conference held in Paris that year, the enthusiastic executives talked about ramping up gas production, not just as a short-term transition fuel to clean energy but as a replacement fuel for coal.

Adding his voice to the chorus in Paris was Woodside's then chief executive, Peter Coleman, who told his colleagues, "Our industry has historically been too timid to aggressively address the shortcomings of coal, but now is the time to stand up and we need to stand united. We, the gas sector, must do more to highlight the benefits of gas over the product of our competitors." And in a dig at Australia's coal industry, he quipped, "Give me a break. Who coined clean coal?"

Coleman's remarks shocked Australia's coal industry and Canberra, but Woodside was making plans to profit from the Paris accord and the decline of coal. The message that gas could help address climate change while enriching the nation was a potent argument for Australian politicians as our fossil-fuel exports soared. When Woodside launched the Burrup Hub gas expansion six years later, that was the key message it seized on to sell the plans to shareholders, the media and the public. It is a message that has been enthusiastically backed by both Labor and the Coalition in both Perth and Canberra. Woodside argues the world needs more of its gas, not less. "We have a very important role to play in helping the world decarbonise," is O'Neill's mantra. She points out that China, India and Southeast Asia are aiming to cut their emissions. "Their energy mix is going to have to change and LNG and gas is going to be an increasingly important part of that mix," she told me. "Gas has half the life-cycle emissions of coal, providing base-load power and offering a complement to renewables." But the emissions footprint of LNG is higher than the industry suggests and, as we will see, its long-term use as a transition fuel is often greatly exaggerated.

While Piers Verstegen accepts that Woodside's Asian customers will need some gas for the energy transition as they move away from coal, he is adamant this doesn't justify Woodside's multi-billion-dollar gas investments when renewable energy is growing rapidly. "What they know is the amount of gas that would be used is a tiny fraction of what they want to export. They're working to preserve their markets and expand their markets."

Woodside's towering headquarters dominates the city skyline when you stand on the steps of the West Australian parliament. It's the first thing I noticed when I met Chris Tallentire there. Tallentire had just retired at the state election in March with some regrets. As a Labor backbencher, he had hoped to see the WA parliament pass a climate change bill that would finally legislate a net-zero emissions target for 2050. Western Australia is the only state without one. The bill never passed, and over lunch in the dining room Tallentire told me he was probably partly to blame. "When we saw the draft bill presented in November 2023," he explained simply, "it had a few weaknesses."

Like Premier Roger Cook, Tallentire is from Labor's Left faction. He was stoked when Cook took over the top job from Mark McGowan in 2023 and pushed ahead with Labor's promised climate bill. But Tallentire put a spanner in the works by suggesting amendments. He wanted experts, like the Albanese government's independent Climate Change Authority, to look at the interim emissions targets on the way to net zero. He wanted their advice based on climate science as well as economic, social and global factors and he wanted it made public. "I felt it was necessary because we kept on being told, 'Don't worry, WA will have to have an increase in its emissions before they go down, but that's going to help Asia reduce its emissions.'"

This argument was being pushed heavily by Cook in the Labor caucus. WA gas was doing the planet a service by decarbonising Asia. Or, as Cook put it, "If not for WA's natural gas, countries such as Japan and South Korea would have no choice but to use more coal." Cook was echoing the gas industry's pitch, which had been run hard since the Paris Agreement. But Cook and his then environment and energy minister, Reece Whitby, also knew Western Australia's LNG industry had been pushing up the state's greenhouse gas emissions – apart from a dip during COVID. Unless it changed course, the state government had no clear pathway to reach net zero by 2050. Complicating matters further, the Albanese government was promising to reduce the nation's greenhouse gas emissions by 43 per cent by 2030, in line with its Paris target. Western Australia wasn't helping this effort.

When Cook unveiled the state's climate change bill, he called for Western Australia to be cut some slack, basically because the state was taking a hit for the team. At a hyped-up Energy Transition Summit in Perth with the federal energy minister, Chris Bowen, and federal resources minister, Madeleine King, Cook laid out a grand plan for Western Australia to play a leading role in the global energy transition by processing and exporting critical minerals, developing green hydrogen and expanding renewable energy, but also by continuing its large LNG exports to Asia. "Put simply, the benefits of WA helping other high-emission countries to decarbonise far outstrips the benefits of decarbonising our own economy," Cook told the summit. "The global transition isn't always as simple as quitting fossil fuels and replacing it with renewables. That would devastate economies, plunge major cities into darkness, and see coal-fired power plants turned back on." Cook insisted that Western Australia's LNG exports to Asia were not competing with renewables, just the opposite: "I want to be clear – this isn't about gas displacing renewable energy sources." He had a "solid commitment" from senior Japanese and Korean officials to switch to more renewable energy. "Their sense of urgency is as great as ours," he promised.

Meg O'Neill backed Cook's argument. "I'll commend him for being so bold with his statements that for WA to play a constructive role in tackling climate change WA emissions may go up as we provide more LNG to help nations in our region meet their decarbonisation goals," she told me, adding it was "very myopic" just to focus on emissions in the state.

A number of Cook's backbenchers weren't convinced by this argument. Tallentire told me he suggested to Cook and Whitby it would be helpful to get some evidence supporting the claim that more gas wouldn't squeeze out renewables in Asia's energy transition. "I can see that's possible, but let's get some real figures on it," he said. At a caucus retreat in February 2024, as the climate change bill began to stall, Tallentire raised the issue again. He said the premier told him, "Yep, don't worry, we'll get you the figures."

But it soon emerged Whitby's department couldn't produce any convincing figures and neither could state Treasury. Finally, Tallentire said, he was told "government doesn't have the expertise to get these figures." An external consultant was suggested to do the report but still no report appeared for the caucus. (Cook's office wouldn't answer my questions about this.) In late 2024, five months out from the state election, Western Australia's climate change bill was shelved.

In May 2025, less than a week after Labor won the federal election, Cook walked back on the bill, saying his state was covered by the federal net-zero target. "I'm not going to shackle Western Australia to legislation which damages our efforts to help the globe to decarbonise and reduce emissions."

When Tallentire first questioned Cook's claims about decarbonising Asia, he wasn't just trying to score a point. In Opposition, Tallentire had been the shadow environment minister and was a former director of the Conservation Council of WA. The questions went to the core of WA's climate and energy policy. Is the gas industry still helping Asia – and Western Australia – get to net-zero emissions by 2050, or is it hindering this? And how do state politicians figure that out independently of the industry and its lobbyists? Experts from the CSIRO all the way to the US Department of Energy have wrestled with the same vexed claims over the last seven years and have raised doubts about the industry's arguments.

The real answer is, of course, complicated. No credible figure in the energy industry is suggesting gas and coal can be replaced overnight, and it's a straw-man argument to raise it. Most analysts believe gas will play a role in backing up renewables and as a feedstock (an input) for some critical industries for several decades. The issue is how much gas, for how long, and can these emissions be credibly offset or captured if global warming is going to stay as close to 1.5°C as possible.

The Albanese government appointed the independent Climate Change Authority to advise on these vexed questions. Last year the CCA put out a report with the clunky title *Sector Pathways Review*. The CCA cited two important studies, the UN's 2022 IPCC report and the 2023 International Energy

Agency Net Zero Roadmap. Both, it said, have concluded that, "globally, new fossil-fuel projects are incompatible with achieving the Paris Agreement goal of limiting warming to 1.5°C, and that global demand for fossil fuels will need to significantly decline over the period to 2050." Both studies found demand for gas will need to drop dramatically by 2050, the IPCC estimating by as much as 62 per cent and the IEA by around 78 per cent.

The CCA's report also made the point that fossil fuels, mainly LNG and coal, account for over a third of Australia's exports, goods and services combined. When our export partners burn these fuels, they produce more than double Australia's domestic greenhouse gas emissions. For Australia to thrive in a net-zero global economy, it will need to change its export mix and work with trading partners, including Japan and Korea, "to manage an orderly transition away from fossil fuels."

By and large, that message does not go down well in Perth. "Japan, Korea and China are entitled to make their own decisions about their pathway. They've all said in public, hundreds of times, that they will need LNG beyond 2050 to meet their carbon targets. To me, that's the end of the debate." That was the lecture I got over coffee from Bill Johnston, the mines, petroleum and energy minister in Mark McGowan's government, who left the job after Cook took over and retired at the last election. Johnston is old-school Labor Right and diligently oversaw Western Australia's giant LNG projects for five years as Woodside powered ahead planning its "carbon bomb" – the Scarborough project and NWS extension and Browse Basin projects. Johnston berated Greenpeace for calling these projects an *expansion* of the gas industry, saying they are needed to *replace* gas from depleting off-shore fields. When I suggested that Western Australia's LNG exports might actually have to shrink dramatically rather than stay steady, if the world is to make the Paris target, Johnston could barely contain his exasperation. "You can't get to 1.5 without LNG exports," he argued. "The Korean and Japanese ministers tell me they cannot meet their carbon emissions targets without Australian LNG. Now, we have to accept that that's true. So therefore Australian LNG exports contribute to our Asian partners meeting their climate targets. They help them *meet* their climate targets, and we know that because they've told us."

Johnston was also adamant that without LNG there wouldn't be sufficient domestic gas supplies in Western Australia, and that, he said, would affect the living standard of every Australian. He dismissed the idea that Western Australia's emissions from its LNG industry are a problem for the rest of Australia. "The idea that every state needs to have the same emissions profile is not possible nor necessary," he said. "It's saying that we aren't one country."

*

When Mark McGowan took over as premier in 2017, Western Australia was heavily in debt and had a falling growth rate and high unemployment. With his treasurer, Ben Wyatt, and energy minister, Johnston, McGowan was laser-focused on jobs and development. Gas, domestic and LNG, was central to their plans. McGowan and Johnston pressed Woodside for a timetable to get the Burrup Hub projects moving. The following year, Woodside, then under CEO Peter Coleman, put the NWS extension proposal to the state's Environmental Protection Agency for approval. The Scarborough project was also looking more promising. In early 2019, the Woodside board hosted a dinner for the premier and it was smiles all round. Just weeks later, McGowan and Woodside went to war with the EPA over greenhouse gas emissions.

Tom Hatton was chair of the EPA at the time and still nurses the scars. Hatton is no radical climate activist. After working for the US forestry service, he spent twenty-five years with the CSIRO before chairing the EPA, an independent body that endeavours to protect the state's environment. The EPA advises the state government on approvals for big projects.

Hatton's relationship with McGowan hit the wall because the EPA board decided to issue new greenhouse gas emissions guidelines for the state's big resources and gas companies. The EPA had long given advice on emissions while taking into account federal government emissions regulations to avoid duplication. But at the time the Morrison government would still not commit to net zero and Australia's emissions had spiked up by 2018, partly driven by LNG production in Western Australia.

"I think we were the only jurisdiction where greenhouse gas emissions were still going up, and they were projected to go up markedly with the new developments on the table, including Woodside's," Hatton explained.

This was a pivotal moment for the WA gas industry. Emissions from LNG projects are large. The industry markets its product as "natural gas," but it's mainly methane – the second-largest greenhouse gas contributor to global warming. When burnt, it produces CO_2 and water vapour and can emit between about half or less the emissions of coal. But the business of extracting the gas from offshore fields, processing and shipping it as LNG is highly emissions-intensive and adds to a large carbon footprint. The latest IEA finding says that when the full life cycle of LNG is considered, on average it results in only 25 per cent less emissions than coal.

Put simply, LNG projects have three types of emissions. Scope 1 come from burning fuel onsite, where huge gas turbines power the refrigeration trains to make LNG, and from methane leaking, which happens during the extraction and processing phases. Scope 2 come from the plants' indirect emissions, such as consuming fuel produced offsite. Both are the responsibility of the project operator. Scope 3 emissions mostly come when the LNG is burnt by the customers, who, in theory, should account for them.

When Hatton and the EPA board put out their emissions guidelines in 2019, the gas industry had seen nothing quite like them in Australia. They said, basically, if your project is going to make more than 100,000 tonnes of greenhouse gas emissions a year, we expect you to show you are using best-practice technologies to minimise emissions. We also want you to estimate your Scope 1 and Scope 2 emissions, and in some cases, at the EPA's discretion, we may ask for estimates of your Scope 3 emissions.

"And then there was the one that got the hackles up," Hatton told me. "Show us why you can't do everything reasonable and practical to offset Scope 1 emissions." Hatton was at pains to explain these were only EPA guidelines – to inform the EPA's advice to the minister. The EPA has no enforcement powers to impose these guidelines on industry. That didn't matter. "We published those guidelines and the reaction by some of the companies was volatile."

Almost immediately, Woodside's boss was on the phone to McGowan's environment minister and, more importantly, to Kerry Stokes' *West Australian* newspaper. *The West* went to town. Its page-one splash was an attack on the EPA board. "Out of Their Mines" it roared, with the kicker line, "Tens of billions of dollars at risk after pen-pushers call for 'net zero' emissions." The story quoted Woodside's Coleman being "quite angry about it," which was, to say the least, an understatement. Coleman penned an op-ed the next day headlined "Premier must fix the EPA's carbon emissions mess." From Canberra, Morrison chimed in, calling the guidelines "unworkable." Woodside took out full-page ads in the newspaper.

The story was huge news in Western Australia. Looking back, Hatton believes the guidelines were being misinterpreted or misrepresented by the companies for a reason. "They did not want the EPA – and they still don't want the EPA – to say anything about greenhouse gas emissions. They don't want them to even be assessed. This was a 'nip it in the bud' thing," he said.

Rocked by the industry response, McGowan called an urgent roundtable with the big emitters, Woodside, Chevron, Santos and Shell, along with Johnston and his environment minister, Stephen Dawson. When it was over, the premier got straight onto Hatton. "Mr McGowan called me out of the blue, immediately coming out of that meeting, saying, 'Tom, I want you to withdraw the guidelines,'" Hatton recalled. "It was maybe eleven o'clock in the morning and he gave me to one o'clock. He said, 'I'm having a press conference at one o'clock and I want your answer.'"

Hatton was stunned. "It was entirely inappropriate because it served to pre-empt the EPA's independent statutory advice to government. EPA guidelines are neither regulation nor government policy. They serve to define the information requested from the proponents and to structure advice to the minister, who may follow that advice or not. That is always the government's prerogative."

After McGowan's call, Hatton and the EPA board went into crisis mode and in the end opted to compromise. The consensus thinking was that while they were legally obliged to use their best efforts to protect the environment, "if we stick to our guns on the guidelines as drafted, we risk making ourselves irrelevant." With the help of Bill Johnston, a compromise was reached that became government policy – but not legislation. It was better than nothing. It resulted in the first statutory conditions on new big emitting projects to gradually reduce their emissions to net zero by 2050. (Even this policy would later be overturned by the Cook government.)

McGowan doesn't talk to reporters now that he is no longer premier, but he told parliament at the time, "The government did not support the guidance because it would unfairly target the LNG industry, which produces less than half the emissions intensity per tonne of CO_2 produced from other forms of fuel." Johnston defended the demand to have the original EPA guidelines withdrawn, saying the EPA had put out the guidelines without first talking to the government. "The government was very keen to make sure that the EPA's advice to industry matched the government's expectation," was how he put it.

For Hatton, the independence of the EPA was put at stake, and he still feels this keenly. "The notion that what is good for large resource companies operating here is always good for WA is deeply embedded in our culture, and not just in our politicians," said Hatton. "The inclination to protect the commercial interests of those companies by compromising the statutory arrangements designed to ensure government decisions are informed by independent, transparent, science-based advice is neither commendable nor in the public interest."

Hatton's concerns are reinforced if you read Stokes' media outlets on a daily basis. They often sound like a loud megaphone for the gas industry and this is not surprising. With his son Ryan, Stokes also has a big stake in the gas industry through Beach Energy.

Stokes' influence over both the McGowan and Cook governments is a hot topic among Labor insiders. "All bravery was knocked out of Cook by

The West," one told me. Stokes' Seven West Media runs *The West Australian* along with the Seven Network, online news sites *The Nightly* and *PerthNow*, *The Sunday Times* and a regional newspaper chain. Seven West's Telethon Ball is Perth's power networking event of the year. As *The Australian Financial Review*'s Mark Di Stefano quipped, "It's an annual dual-purpose social event that raises millions of dollars for sick kids, while also functioning as a transparent attempt by the nation's elite to bend the knee to the state's kingmaker." He reported an incident in 2022 when then Perth lord mayor and Telethon Ball host Basil Zempilas joked to the crowd, which included Premier McGowan and Prime Minister Albanese, "I also want to thank Kerry – the man who really runs the state." Zempilas, a Seven West employee for years, is now the Liberal Party leader in Western Australia.

The chair of Seven's Telethon Trust is Woodside's chairman, Richard Goyder. He and Stokes rub shoulders at the AFL, where Goyder is chairman and Seven has the free-to-air television rights to the game. More than a decade ago, Stokes hired a former Woodside CEO, Don Voelte, who built up his investment in Beach Energy, an onshore gas company which now has ambitions to be an industry leader in Australia.

When McGowan was still premier, his relationship with Stokes came under scrutiny when a Beach Energy project appeared to get special treatment from the Labor government. In 2020, McGowan unveiled a crucial update of the state's domestic gas reservation policy that banned the export of gas from Western Australia's onshore fields. The ban was prompted in part by Woodside's NWS plant, which had begun touting for new suppliers to fill the big LNG trains at the Karratha plant because of the depleting stocks of gas from its offshore fields. McGowan made one exception to the new ban: the Waitsia project in the Perth Basin, jointly owned by Stokes' Beach Energy and Japan's Mitsui. Citing the "exceptional economic circumstances" created by the COVID-19 crisis, McGowan said the state was allowing Waitsia to export half its gas through to 2028 using the Woodside-operated Karratha gas plant. Both McGowan and Stokes denied there had been any direct discussions between the two over the deal; McGowan said simply that the Waitsia project wouldn't stand up financially without the right to export. This was no doubt true, but the Waitsia exemption was widely perceived as reflecting the weight given to Stokes' views on the state's gas policy. Cook has since updated the policy, allowing other onshore producers to export one-fifth of their gas until 2030.

*

To an outsider, the power of the gas industry in Western Australia is extraordinary, but it would be a mistake to see it as lacking broad support. The state's industrial base is built on gas and it has big-union as well as big-business backing. While gas lobbyists love to talk about natural gas "keeping the lights on" and "keeping people warm," the reality in Western Australia is that, even though gas dominates the power system, less than 8 per cent of domestic gas goes to homes and small businesses. The biggest consumers are minerals processors like Alcoa, and the mining industry, followed by fertiliser, chemical and explosives plants.

"Western Australia's domestic gas is largely used for industrial purposes where there is currently no viable alternative and renewable energy is not currently an option," Johnston insists. For politicians, especially Labor ones like Johnston, McGowan and Cook, gas means blue-collar jobs in influential unions, including the Australian Workers' Union and the Maritime Union of Australia. For the most part, they can't see gas in industry being replaced by large-scale renewables in a major way anytime soon – even if they are backed up by gas and big batteries. While the Cook government has great plans for renewables in Western Australia and is making progress decarbonising its electricity grid, analysts I spoke to said the state is not willing to put up enough money to support a broad energy transition across industry that would cost tens of billions of dollars.

"Just like in every part of the country, for Western Australia's domestic gas supply the transition is not the next two years, it's not the next five years, it's the next twenty years and probably thirty years," is Bill Johnston unshakeable view. Western Australia is not going to bet the farm on becoming a renewable energy superpower – despite the rhetoric on renewables and green hydrogen coming from Albanese. Apart from outliers like Fortescue's chairman Andrew Forrest, who vocally promotes industry decarbonisation, gas dominates the energy debate in WA business and Labor circles. That debate is getting hotter with the state's ageing coal-fired generators set to shut down by 2030.

According to Johnston, this is when gas supply "falls off a cliff." A recent state parliamentary inquiry rang alarm bells about a gas shortage in Western Australia after 2030. The inquiry's report was a rallying cry to open up more fields and back in Woodside's big projects. The dire warnings of Western Australia's future domestic gas shortage reinforced the Cook government's support for Woodside's new projects. To every economic problem in Western Australia, it can seem that the answer is "more gas."

When Woodside originally argued its case for Scarborough and the NWS extension, it used the same arguments. Back then, Piers Verstegen was still head of the Conservation Council of WA. He believed that stopping Woodside's new projects was the most important climate campaign facing the country. He and a group of like-minded colleagues were determined to fight the state and federal approvals for the projects. Their campaign began in the west but ultimately became a national movement to tear up Woodside's social licence and turn Australia's LNG export trade into the nation's biggest environmental issue.

Shortly after 10.30 pm on a cold winter night in Perth in 2023, a Toyota Hilux cruised by Meg O'Neill's swish house in City Beach, one of the city's more upmarket oceanfront suburbs. Behind the wheel was a young climate activist, Emil Davey, who was doing a recce on the place. Suddenly, an unmarked car pulled up in front of him. A man leapt out with a gun, pointed it at Davey's face through the windscreen and shouted at him. Davey completely freaked. The man, it turned out, was a plain-clothes cop; he went on to search Davey's car before releasing him without charge. Unbeknown to Davey, he had unwittingly driven straight into Operation Frederick. Western Australia's State Security Investigation Group, part of the anti-terrorism police, was targeting Disrupt Burrup Hub activists. They were expecting Davey's friends to descend on O'Neill's house early next morning.

Sure enough, around sunrise the activists pulled up outside the house, followed by a crew from the ABC's *Four Corners*. In the car was Matilda Lane-Rose, nineteen, a veteran of the School Strike 4 Climate campaign. She was psyched up to splash and spray yellow paint on O'Neill's fence and garage, then bike-lock herself to the gate. Her fellow activist, videographer Gerard Mazza, was there to record her social media plea to stop Woodside's gas projects. But before Mazza could set up his lights on the driveway, armed police descended on them. "Police! Don't move! Don't move!" From an upstairs window O'Neill looked down on the scene as chaos erupted. Her teenage daughter was also inside the house.

In the street, Disrupt Burrup Hub's media strategist, Jesse Noakes, was still sitting in the car when he saw the police coming. "We thought she [O'Neill] wasn't going to be there," Noakes told me later. "The first I knew was a loud shout like, 'Stop! Police!' They came racing out of the front gate." Noakes, with the others, was arrested, taken away and charged with conspiracy to commit an indictable office. Davey was picked up later and also charged.

I asked Noakes: how did the police know about the activists' plans? "I can very confidently state that information came from an operative placed within the Disrupt Burrup Hub campaign for the purpose of feeding information back to police," he said. "They had been revealing information to police that led to their pre-emptive knowledge of multiple protests."

At first glance, the action at O'Neill's house looked like a PR disaster for Disrupt Burrup Hub. The Woodside CEO was no longer Methane Meg but a victim, despite the activists insisting she was never in danger from a nineteen-year-old with a spray can. When I asked O'Neill about that morning, she was clearly still upset about it. "It was absolutely distressing for myself and my family members. The one real positive that we took away as a family from the event was the strong condemnation for the protesters by politicians from both sides of the aisle, and the strong condemnation from members of the community," she said. "Hopefully that's been a real clear message to the radical movement that intimidating family members and people in the industry is not acceptable, and it's not acceptable to members of the Australian public at large."

Business leaders and politicians around the country, including Labor's Chris Bowen and Madeleine King, slammed the activists. "This is beyond the pale to go to someone's house," said King. The Liberals' Michaelia Cash demanded a Senate inquiry into *Four Corners*' involvement – it was making a program on the protesters. Woodside lodged an official complaint with the ABC. Premier Roger Cook wrote to the ABC's chairwoman, Ita Buttrose, saying, "Wittingly or unwittingly, the ABC was complicit." The ABC's managing director, David Anderson, sent a letter of regret to O'Neill when Sky News aired CCTV images of the ABC crew on O'Neill's driveway – albeit outside her gate. A few weeks later O'Neill upped the ante, taking out restraining orders against Noakes, Mazza, Lane-Rose and Davey that included gagging them from posting or talking about her online. The order was scaled back a few months later, but not dropped.

Noakes was not overly worried by the negative publicity. For him, the high-profile protest at O'Neill's house was the climax of an eight-month campaign to focus national media attention on Woodside's new projects. "The Disrupt Burrup Hub campaign was always conceived of as a branding campaign, first and foremost. It was intended to put the Burrup Hub on the map," he told me. "It was more successful than I could have anticipated or expected, and of course *Four Corners* was the primary fulcrum for that." The protest at O'Neill's house, he said, "played into the narrative that we have been seeking to expose and highlight, which is the degree of collusion between Woodside, the WA government and their instruments – state capture, to use that sanitised term."

The campaign was in tune with a global upsurge in climate radicalism after the Paris Agreement. While direct action has long been used by Greenpeace against specific targets like fishing trawlers and nuclear plants, the new wave of climate protests set out to disrupt closer to home – commuters on freeways, workers at fossil-fuel plants, CEOs and directors at their AGMs, spectators at sports stadiums, and visitors to art galleries. Six months before Disrupt Burrup Hub kicked off in Perth, a likeminded British outfit, Just Stop Oil, had gone to London's National Gallery and taped a bleak picture of environmental destruction over John Constable's bucolic painting *The Hay Wain*, before gluing their hands to the frame and awaiting arrest.

The Disrupt Burrup Hub campaign worked at arm's length from Australia's mainstream environment groups and did things they couldn't. "It was a renegade action against a very powerful state," said Noakes. "Basically, all the initial activity was driven by a dozen people. A small team, deliberately tight. And that didn't require hundreds and hundreds of people on the street. It required high-profile stunts, effectively involving small numbers of people doing some fairly innovative, escalatory things that drew a response out of the state."

Their first stunt was at the Art Gallery of Western Australia in January 2023, when Joana Partyka sprayed the Woodside logo in yellow paint on the Perspex covering Frederick McCubbin's colonial painting *Down on His Luck*. (The protest was later approved by some of McCubbin's descendants.) The following month, a punk musician, Trent Rojahn, frontman for Last Quokka, used a fire extinguisher full of yellow paint to spray "Disrupt Burrup Hub" on the entrance to Woodside's headquarters. Soon after, graphic designer Tahlia Stolarski sprayed the Woodside logo in yellow paint on the entrance of the WA parliament. Then, in April, came Woodside's 2023 AGM, when Mazza, Stolarski and Noakes were charged with aggravated burglary over attempting to disrupt the meeting with a stink bomb. That June, activist Kristen Morrissey forced the evacuation of some 1600 workers from Woodside's corporate headquarters using a stink bomb to simulate a gas leak. By then, Woodside and O'Neill had had enough. In late June, Woodside's lawyers issued threats to sue Morrissey and a fellow Disrupt Burrup Hub activist in the WA Supreme Court for loss of earnings and brand damage. This prompted the Greens' federal deputy leader, Senator Mehreen Faruqi, to denounce Woodside as "a corporate villain, pure and simple. They are destroying the planet, reaping billions in profits, they have the Labor and Liberal parties wrapped around their fingers and now they are trying to bankrupt two women who dared challenge their dangerous expansion plans." Weeks later, Disrupt Burrup Hub targeted O'Neill's house.

One of the activists' aims was to provoke a backlash from the state, but the group quickly became a victim of their own success. They were shocked when they were hit with armed police raids, criminal charges and search and seizure orders, along with threatening civil orders from Woodside. "It's definitely the case that people have been exhausted, intimidated and traumatised by the response they received," Noakes conceded, "not least by the fact that once you get over the initial shock of arrests and the raids and the charges, you then have to spend an indefinite period of time coming into court every four to six weeks."

The hardline response should have been expected. The WA Labor government had joined Queensland and New South Wales in a nationwide crackdown on climate activists, a move long lobbied for by coal and gas companies in Australia and in other Western countries. In the UK, protesters with Just Stop Oil and Extinction Rebellion were being sentenced to prison. Roger Cook made no apology for using counterterrorism police to target activists. "Everyone is entitled to protest peacefully in WA," he said through a spokesperson. "However, police will act when it comes to violent or threatening behaviour."

At the WA Supreme Court, I met up with lawyer Zarah Burgess, who represented several of the activists and was quick to point out there was no evidence of violent behaviour at their protests. Burgess, who knows her way around the criminal courts, calls her climate activist clients "my ragamuffins." She was surprised to see the involvement of the State Security police. "That unit, in my experience, is there to deal with counterterrorism measures, outlaw motorcycle gangs and [far-]right-wing groups. They're there for pretty serious stuff. I have never before seen them engaged for climate activists."

Burgess believes the involvement of State Security police saw the usual range of trespass and civil disobedience offences against the protesters bumped up to more serious criminal offences. She called it "overcharging" and said it gave the police much wider search and seizure powers, especially the power to serve broad data-access orders. "This has been a big thing," she explained. "They've been served on protesters to compel them to give police access to their phones, laptops, electronic devices. We've been to trial for not obeying the data-access orders." By the time the activists who went to O'Neill's house finally got to court, the charges had been downgraded to attempted trespass and attempted unlawful damage on the fence and garage door of the property. They were fined a few thousand dollars each. But more recently, the courts have been less lenient. The two activists involved in the hoax to evacuate Woodside's headquarters, Morrissey and Partyka, were given suspended prison sentences of eleven and seven months.

Another lawyer advising the Disrupt Burrup Hub activists, Julia Grix, who today runs Climate Defenders Australia, told me she thought the data-access orders slapped on protesters by WA police were likely for surveillance purposes and to intimidate them. "It was arguably a punitive exercise rather than merely investigative," she said. "It seemed, in my opinion, designed to scare them off from taking action, to silence them and shut them down." Noakes also told me the legal advice sent to him by the Environmental Defenders Office was obtained by the police informant inside Disrupt Burrup Hub and used against them: "[The police] cited it as grounds for further searches and seizures of devices, which may well be a breach of legal privilege."

*

While Disrupt Burrup Hub looked like a renegade group, its members often had links to the mainstream environmental movement and their actions were in no small part designed to fire up the broader anti-Woodside campaign. "Really, Disrupt Burrup Hub was effectively a response to a bit of a void in traditional campaign resources," said Noakes. In fact, it was a way to ignite a larger campaign. When O'Neill greenlit the Scarborough project in November 2021, the big east-coast-based environmental groups had few staff in the west and initial campaigning against Woodside got limited traction. That would change dramatically.

The state's peak environment group, the Conservation Council of WA, had enlisted the Environmental Defenders Office to try to stop Woodside's Scarborough project in the state Supreme Court but lost that case in February 2022, leaving the CCWA depleted of funds. David Ritter, at Greenpeace's head office in Sydney, told me he was approached to get involved around this time. "What the WA Conservation Council said to us was, 'Woodside is this global-scale leviathan. Look at the emissions that will be generated from this one project. So how about it, Greenpeace?'"

Greenpeace made a splashy entrance to the campaign that September with the help of Peter Garrett and Midnight Oil, who were doing a farewell concert in Perth. Ritter was in the audience of 11,000 fans when, halfway through the gig, Garrett changed into a Greenpeace t-shirt with "Woodside = Climate Wrecker" emblazoned on the front. A giant projection lit up the stage behind him with the words "Woodside Ecocide" and a graphic of a large hand holding up the Earth on fire. Garrett said he was later told that Ben Wyatt, who had been appointed to the Woodside board, was in the audience when he called out, "Why is Woodside, this company, wanting to produce so much poisonous gas?"

When Disrupt Burrup Hub kicked off a few months later, national media interest in Woodside ticked up. Greenpeace hired a new organiser for its Perth team, Sophie McNeill, an ex–*Four Corners* reporter, human rights worker and Perth native. McNeill set about challenging Woodside's big cultural influence in Perth, where the company is a lavish sponsor of everything from music to sport, including the Nippers and the AFL's Fremantle Dockers team, a textbook case of corporate soft power.

"I'd try to talk to people about Woodside and how nuts it was," McNeill complained. "They're on the back of a kids' rashie as they run around and do their surf lifesaving. They're on my football team. It's bad enough being a Dockers' supporter, because we're, like, one of the least successful teams in the AFL, let alone as a climate activist. You're having to endure seeing your favourite team have Woodside plastered all over them. And people are, like, 'What are you talking about? What's wrong with Woodside?'" McNeill began a "Free the Nippers" campaign with a local doctor and worked on a petition to kill off Woodside's Dockers sponsorship. Carmen Lawrence, who described McNeill as "a force of nature," joined her and Josie Alec, the Australian Conservation Foundation's lead Indigenous organiser, on the Dockers campaign. Meg O'Neill thwarted their efforts and kept the Dockers club on board with Woodside. The Nippers also kept their sponsorship.

Greenpeace had a lot more success with a campaign to hammer Woodside over its controversial plans to drill offshore in the Browse Basin, some 425 kilometres north of Broome. The Greenpeace campaign focused on one of the key drilling areas just 3 kilometres from Scott Reef, a stunning, richly diverse coral reef system that lies in both state and federal waters. For years, gas companies had commissioned studies on the reef, no doubt hoping to reassure state and federal authorities that their plans would not endanger the fragile ecosystem which includes Sandy Islet, a critical nesting site for endangered green sea turtles. Woodside has said it will put a 20-kilometre buffer between the islet and any drilling site, which has not reassured environmental campaigners. The surrounding waters are also foraging areas for migrating humpback and blue pygmy whales.

The day before Woodside's raucous 2023 AGM, Greenpeace sailed its *Rainbow Warrior* ship into Fremantle Harbour and later up the west coast to Scott Reef, where its campaigners took evocative shots of turtles on the beach. Meanwhile, back in Perth, Greenpeace kicked off its guerilla ad campaign, "Woodside's War on Whales." All this got traction. By 2024, it was clear Scott Reef was a problem for Woodside and its Browse partners. One of Western Australia's best-informed gas industry reporters, Peter Milne, revealed that the WA EPA had written to Woodside questioning its plans to drill so close to the reef and the sensitive nesting site. It also questioned Woodside's response plans for containing a catastrophic blow-out spill during drilling operations – something Woodside's engineers insisted had a minuscule chance of happening.

Woodside's Browse applications to the federal and state governments are, technically, separate from its applications to extend the NWS gas plant. As O'Neill put it, "The approval for the North West Shelf's life extension has nothing to do with Browse, it's about continuing to operate facilities that are in place today." But in 2024 Greenpeace kept making the point that Woodside and its partners wanted the new gas from the Browse fields to feed the NWS plant through to 2070. Strategically, Greenpeace was asking the federal environment minister, Tanya Plibersek, to block the NWS extension because of Woodside's plans in the Browse, which would damage Scott Reef. "Browse is the one where you have this filthy deposit, you have it next to Scott Reef. So, logically, it's the one that is most amenable to be stopped," Ritter told me. By the winter of 2024, Greenpeace had gathered 440,000 e-signatures on a petition, which it delivered to Plibersek at Parliament House. During the handover, Greenpeace campaigners rolled out a giant scroll on the front lawn, on it a mock-up of the 440,000 names calling on the minister "To protect our precious environment from Woodside's Burrup Hub."

*

The long, hectic campaign brought the Burrup Hub gas plans to national attention, mobilised environment groups on the east coast and put the climate movement's case against the company to federal politicians. But none of this stopped Woodside forging ahead with its strategy. O'Neill stared down every challenge as it arose. What all the actions exposed was a fundamental weakness at the heart of the campaign. It is almost impossible to legally challenge Woodside on the very issue the environment groups are most concerned about, the huge greenhouse gas emissions created by Woodside's new developments on the Burrup not just at home but globally: the NWS extension, the planned Browse gas wells and the Scarborough gas project.

Climate change driven by rising greenhouse gas emissions is the greatest long-term threat to Australia's natural environment, but the national environmental protection laws, the *Environment Protection and Biodiversity Conservation (EPBC) Act*, are virtually mute on the subject. For this reason, the Australian Conservation Foundation decided one of its key roles in the Burrup Hub campaign would be to try to challenge Woodside in the Federal Court. It wanted to use the case to test the limits of the *EPBC Act* when it came to new fossil-fuel developments. It hired the Environmental Defenders Office to take on the case and briefed a senior counsel.

The ACF case rested on the claim that Woodside's Scarborough project is so big that its emissions would measurably add to global warming and further damage the Great Barrier Reef, which has already suffered mass coral bleaching in recent years. For this reason, the ACF argued, the federal court should block Woodside's Scarborough project until it is assessed under the *EPBC Act* – putting the approval for the Scarborough onto the environment minister's desk. If the ACF won the case, it would mean a major fossil-fuel project's impact on climate change might finally be assessed under Australia's environment laws.

Critical to the ACF's argument was that the total lifetime emissions of Scarborough included not only the emissions created by Woodside producing the LNG in Australia at its expanded Pluto plant, but also the emissions created by its customers in Japan, China and Korea burning the gas for several decades. Using this framework, the ACF estimated Scarborough's lifetime emissions at equal to about three years of Australia's total annual emissions.

I asked Kelly O'Shanassy, the ACF's head, why they put their money and resources into what looked like a moonshot case. "The *EPBC Act* is pretty broken and ministers are using it to approve great big, mega-polluting coal and gas mines," she explained. "They are saying they don't have any legal requirements in the Act to consider the climate pollution from these mines in their decision-making and, in particular, the climate pollution that occurs outside of Australia, which is the vast majority of the climate impact of these proposals. When the law is so broken and the governments are not protecting nature, you need to do what you can to fight back against that."

To drum up support for its campaign, the ACF collaborated with Piers Verstegen to examine Woodside's Burrup Hub projects. This led to the provocative "carbon bomb" report released in March 2024. Carbon bombs, Verstegen explained, are defined as fossil-fuel projects that will produce over one billion tonnes of carbon pollution in their lifetime. His report called Woodside's Burrup projects "a climate disaster in the making."

O'Shanassy now admits the case against Woodside was a big call. In August 2024, just months after the "carbon bomb" report was released, the ACF pulled out days before the case was due to be heard. O'Shanassy insisted a technical glitch stopped it going ahead, but it looked like the emissions data were so complicated it was difficult, if not impossible, to nail down for the court hearing and the ACF would face huge costs if it lost. For Woodside, it meant the last serious legal threat to Scarborough from the climate campaign was over.

The ACF directed its energies back to the political battle of reforming the *EPBC Act*, joining the call by Greenpeace and the Greens for a "climate trigger" to be included in the overhaul of the Act. A climate trigger would be a mechanism to force big fossil-fuel projects like Scarborough to be assessed on their greenhouse impact by making climate change a matter of national environmental significance. Albanese and his cabinet were determined that this would not happen on their watch, and so too was the WA gas industry, backed by Roger Cook and media baron Kerry Stokes.

But before that political fight could play out, Woodside and both governments had to contain a turbulent campaign over the impact of the Burrup Hub projects on one of the most important Indigenous heritage sites in Australia.

WORKS OF HUMAN CREATIVE GENIUS

The sun was setting as I walked from the car park to the start of the Deep Gorge trail on the Burrup Peninsula. The local Indigenous people call this place Nganjarli. The short trail, with viewing platforms and a boardwalk, is part of a national park co-managed by the Murujuga Aboriginal Corporation and the West Australian government. I'd timed my arrival perfectly. The late-afternoon light made it easier to spot the famous rock art engravings, half-hidden in the high piles of deep-red boulders. Within minutes I was gazing at a graphic image of a thylacine – a Tasmanian tiger – which roamed here millennia ago, before being driven south and then to extinction. The last one is thought to have died in 1936 in the Hobart Zoo, a long way from its Burrup ancestors.

Tens of thousands of years ago, Indigenous artists came to this remote northwest landscape and created these extraordinary images. They painstakingly pecked, scraped and pounded into the surface of the hard rocks with stone tools and infinite patience. As I stood admiring their work, the dull roar of industry behind me never stopped. From one end of the trail, I could see the tower of Woodside's Pluto gas plant perched on the ridge, a flare burning against a blue sky. Below it, squat in the tidal valley between the hills, sat one of the largest ammonia production sites on Earth, the gas-fed Yara fertiliser plant. Nearby was Yara's chemical plant, along with fresh construction works for a renewable hydrogen project. Underscoring it all was the grind of bulldozers and heavy trucks just a kilometre away, flattening the site of the new Perdaman fertiliser plant soon to be fuelled by Woodside's Scarborough gas. One of the greatest rock art landscapes on Earth is hemmed in by a massive industrial zone.

The clash of Indigenous and white history on the Burrup is brutal and instructive. Every stage of development here has come at the expense of Indigenous cultural heritage, inflicting some lasting damage. Too few Australians know that the Indigenous name for the combined Burrup Peninsula and Dampier Archipelago is Murujuga, or that it's home to one of the densest concentrations of rock art on Earth, estimated at one to two million engravings – petroglyphs – spread over thousands of hectares. Yet for decades archaeologists have hailed these works as one of the most important collections of hunter-forager images in the world, some dating back over 50,000 years, many carved before the last ice age. They include some of the first-known haunting images of ancient faces, along with depictions of spirits, fat-tailed kangaroos, birds, snakes, fish, turtles, emus, crayfish and long-extinct animals. The cultural landscape also holds a rich store of middens, quarries, fish traps, graves, artefacts and stone arrangements marking places where ceremonies have taken place down through the ages.

At the time of white settlement, much of Murujuga was the land of the Yaburara people, until they were decimated by disease and a slaughter known as the Flying Foam Massacre in 1868. Today the Ngarda-Ngarli people are recognised as the Traditional Custodians of this place. They see Murujuga as sacred Country and the rock art as a link to ancestral beings, connected to their lives today by customs and law. They are represented by the Murujuga Aboriginal Corporation.

MAC's head office sits on a road below Woodside's huge Pluto gas plant. When I visited in May 2025, construction of the new LNG train to process the Scarborough gas was going gangbusters, cranes soaring against the skyline. One of MAC's Indigenous rangers, Sarah Hicks, ushered me into the quiet of the boardroom and patiently took me through MAC's cultural awareness program, explaining the work of the local people to preserve Murujuga's unique heritage. The program stresses protecting Country but also preserving unity among MAC's members. "We all come together for Country" was the overriding message in video soundbites from MAC's directors and the Circle of Elders who advise them. At the end of the session, I was told that MAC's chairman, Peter Hicks, was still refusing to talk to me about Woodside and the Burrup developments. I was left to contemplate his video grab about extremists and political groups "dividing our people." I figured that was because MAC's unity had really been put to the test when Woodside started work on its big new Burrup plans.

MAC includes people from five different language groups from the wider Pilbara, who have, at times, fiercely disagreed over how to protect Murujuga's heritage and live with the corporate behemoths that now dominate the Burrup. Not surprisingly, the WA government and the gas industry have long been wary about these groups forging alliances with "greenies" to protect Murujuga. After Labor's Mark McGowan was elected premier, he made a bold move to reach out to the local Indigenous leaders. He promised MAC's then chief executive, Peter Jeffries, he would support a bid for Murujuga to get UNESCO World Heritage listing. His pledge followed an extraordinary four-day World Heritage summit held in the Pilbara town of Karratha, attended by international and local archaeologists, MAC's directors and Elders, along with Jeffries and Carmen Lawrence. All wanted the listing.

McGowan's decision was a big call back in 2018, one his state and Woodside had resisted for years. If listed, the petroglyphs would be recognised under UNESCO's criteria as works of "human creative genius" and Murujuga's cultural landscape would be placed alongside the Chauvet-Pont-d'Arc cave in southern France, home of the famous cave paintings. It would also strengthen the obligation of the WA and federal governments to protect the rock art and the rest of Murujuga's cultural landscape, which is why local Indigenous groups and archaeologists have lobbied so hard for it. The Albanese government announced in 2023 that Canberra would also support the nomination of Murujuga.

Mark McGowan's decision to back the World Heritage campaign turned out to be a double-edged sword for climate activists. While they supported the listing, the activists and several prominent rock-art specialists argued it was completely inconsistent with the new gas developments on the Burrup. "I wish it all the best, but I do worry as to how you can ram a World Heritage nomination through while at the same time allowing major industrial developments right in the middle of the site," UWA professor of archaeology Benjamin Smith told me. "I think the two are in contradiction."

Like the climate activists, Smith argues the Burrup companies' industrial emissions, as distinct from their greenhouse gas emissions, have been, and still are, damaging the rock art, and the new developments will likely increase the problem. These industrial emissions include nitrogen dioxide coming from Woodside's huge Karratha and Pluto gas plants, according to the National Pollutant Inventory. Other pollutants, ammonia and sulphur dioxide, come from the array of industries on the Burrup, including the Yara fertiliser plant, Rio Tinto's Dampier salt plant and the bulk carriers that ship their products and Rio's massive iron-ore exports out through the Dampier port.

Both state and federal governments and the companies argue there is no scientific consensus that today's industrial emissions are having a long-term impact on the rock art. Critically, government approvals for the operations on the Burrup rely heavily on this being so. Over the years, the companies have taken significant steps to cut their industrial emissions and recent improvements in global fuel standards for bulk carriers have also made a difference. But when Murujuga was backed for World Heritage listing in 2018, the threats from industry, in particular industrial emissions, were thrust into the political spotlight.

For the Murujuga Aboriginal Corporation this was a hugely sensitive issue. As the voice of the Traditional Custodians, MAC led the campaign for the World Heritage listing. But as well as having more than 1200 Indigenous members, MAC is financially supported by Woodside and the other companies on the Burrup – Rio Tinto, Yara and Perdaman. These companies helped finance MAC's World Heritage work to support the listing, its consultants, its rangers and its community work. The companies also help finance and advise on the vital Murujuga Rock Art Monitoring Program, which is currently running a $29-million study on the industrial pollution and its impact on the petroglyphs. While the program is conducted by Curtin University, it's overseen by MAC and the WA government's environment department.

When the battle between Woodside and climate activists over the new gas developments ramped up in 2021, the campaign for Murujuga's World Heritage listing was, inevitably, swept up in it. Woodside had made clear that its support for the listing was only "on the basis that heritage and industry can and will continue to co-exist" on the Burrup. Archaeologists and local Indigenous people who had fought for decades to protect the rock art became deeply divided over the climate activists' campaign, with some fearing it could jeopardise the World Heritage listing and MAC's funding. They all knew Woodside had a history of getting what it wanted and that those who lined up against the company and its clients were likely to find themselves on the losing side.

That's pretty much what happened to Dr Ken Mulvaney. Mulvaney lives in an old house nestled above the Dampier port. From his veranda you can watch an endless line of rail cars rattle by, filled with iron ore from the Pilbara on its way to China. When I dropped in one Sunday morning, he graciously offered me a seat with a view. But the celebrated rock-art specialist indicated he did not want to answer my questions about his career-ending fallout with Murujuga's leaders after he objected to the new developments on the Burrup.

Now in his late sixties, Mulvaney is a recognised expert on the Murujuga petroglyphs. In 2022, he was also the principal cultural heritage officer with Rio Tinto, liaising with MAC and Jeffries, then MAC's chief executive. Jeffries abruptly cut ties with Mulvaney for reasons that were never explained, but the split came after the archaeologist was believed to have helped dissident MAC members who were trying to stop the new Perdaman fertiliser plant. Perdaman is Woodside's biggest domestic customer for its Scarborough gas. Word of Jeffries' breach with Mulvaney reached Rio Tinto. Soon after, Mulvaney quietly resigned from his dream job there. His break with MAC's leadership effectively meant he could no longer work on Murujuga.

While Mulvaney batted away these painful events, he was willing to talk about his fraught history with Woodside. Mulvaney came to the Burrup back in 1980, when he was asked to join the hectic archaeological rescue job on Woodside's first construction site for the giant NWS plant. Sir Charles Court's WA government had given an industrial development approval over the area which would lead to the removal of five million tonnes of rock.

Both state and federal ministers knew at the time that the area was rich in Indigenous heritage. Untold numbers of ancient petroglyphs were carved on rocks in the planned construction zone that spread over 200 hectares. The registrar of Aboriginal sites in Western Australia at the time, Bruce Wright, negotiated with Woodside to allow white heritage specialists to record and relocate thousands of the petroglyphs. Some seventeen specialists, many like Mulvaney from the Western Australian Museum, came up in teams to work on what Woodside described as "the biggest heritage salvage effort in Australia's history." Mulvaney described it a bit differently. "The original team was four people, literally working in front of bulldozers to get to record them [the petroglyphs] before they were destroyed."

Mulvaney remembered trying to save what they could. "We were salvaging some rock art," he said. "It was more what we could get, a random scientific sample, rather than just the best. Some rocks were just too big for what equipment we had at the time to lift them."

The white heritage teams were hamstrung by a WA government edict not to officially engage with the local Indigenous people, even though the area was still used by them. "They didn't want us talking to Aboriginal people. We were government employees. So very strict rules, even though we had some Aboriginal staff working with us." While the museum staff forged their own connections with some of the Elders, who told them the stories of the Country, Mulvaney believed the lack of formal negotiations made it difficult for the whites to grasp the cultural significance of what was being destroyed.

"It became absolutely apparent how dense, how diverse and how culturally significant, archeologically, it was, [but] we didn't have the Aboriginal cultural side of it – just how important this place was. This art was reflecting cultural practices over tens of thousands of years. Part of that cultural practice is the sacredness of places, where certain features or places are associated with certain totemic animals and plants and so the rock art will reflect that."

Woodside vice-president Daniel Thomas would later apologise for cutting Indigenous people out of the salvage operation: "It was considered best practice at the time but, regrettably, the Traditional Custodians were excluded from that – something that's no longer acceptable."

By the end of that first salvage operation with Woodside, which spread over 13 square kilometres, the WA Museum had recorded 720 significant heritage sites and 9744 petroglyph panels. "Over 1700 were, we'd say, 'salvaged' – removed from destruction. Some 4000 remained in situ," Mulvaney recalled. I asked what happened to the rest. "Literally bulldozed and smashed up in the gravel to use in construction," he said. "About 5000. To put that in perspective, a lot of countries in the world don't even have that much rock art."

In an essay he wrote about his small part in the building of the Karratha gas plant, Mulvaney summed up his distress at what happened back then: "A lasting impression gained by all concerned was that of the needless annihilation of cultural heritage and landscapes taking place … Such disregard for Australia's cultural heritage was soul-destroying for the archaeologists and Traditional Owners."

*

Four decades later, I am on the phone to local Indigenous woman Raelene Cooper as she pours out her fury over what is happening now on the Burrup. "At the end of the day, what I know is everything you have on the Burrup is a cash cow. And, don't take this disrespectfully, it's a cash cow for white people who come and destroy – and white companies who come and destroy – our history and our culture."

A passionate woman, Cooper is from the Mardudhunera group, one of the five represented by MAC. A director on the MAC board for years, Cooper once served as its chair before her bitter break with MAC's leadership over the gas developments. That came in 2021, not long after her first meeting with "the XR mob" as she called them, climate activists Jesse Noakes, Gerard Mazza and a handful of others who drove up from Perth to Karratha to push their campaign against the Woodside and Perdaman plans. It was spring and they camped out in her Aunty Josie Alec's backyard. By the time they finished talking, Cooper said she was in tears. She knew about the new projects from board meetings but had little grasp of their impact. "When they were telling us about the projects, I was bawling, Mum Josie was bawling, my sister's bawling. We were actually freaking out, because, being someone who sits on the board, I had no idea about it, and the thought of those projects going ahead, really, it was not great to hear it."

Cooper and Alec took the provocative step of forging an alliance with the "greenies." When Meg O'Neill announced the go-ahead for the Scarborough gas project that November, the climate activists returned to Karratha. Before dawn the next morning, three of them blocked the only road onto the Burrup Peninsula with a car and a caravan, cementing their arms into barrels mounted inside their vehicles. One, Petrina Harley, announced she was there to "stand with Traditional Custodians and shut down Scarborough Gas." For twelve hours they cut off access to Australia's largest LNG plant and the Dampier port. Specialist police were flown from Perth to handle the crisis. Cooper found herself in the middle of a "shitshow."

"It was a hell day for me," she remembered. "And while this was all happening, the police weren't allowing our Elders or anyone to go over to the rest of the protesters to help and assist with them, support them. They blocked our Elders to go out there."

When MAC held its annual general meeting days after the protest, tempers frayed. Cooper confronted Peter Jeffries, demanding to know who had given approval for the Woodside and Perdaman projects. Accusations flew, police arrived, and the meeting was shut down. Cooper and Alec decided to set up a breakaway Indigenous group, Save Our Songlines (SOS), with the help of the activists and advice from Piers Verstegen, who was then still with the Conservation Council of WA. Cooper insisted SOS was not "black cladding" for the activists; she wanted to challenge the gas expansion on Indigenous heritage grounds. In the eyes of some in MAC's leadership, Cooper, a MAC director, had crossed the line.

The Save Our Songlines campaign rattled MAC by challenging it as a guardian of Murujuga's cultural heritage, but, as one observer at the meeting told me, Cooper became too bold too late. She hadn't grasped back then that Woodside and Perdaman had been working closely with MAC's leaders for well over two years as the companies prepared to launch their billion-dollar projects. MAC had no real power to stop developments on the Burrup's industrial land. Its only leverage was its standing as the principal voice on Murujuga's heritage, but there was no doubt the power in those negotiations lay with Woodside and Perdaman.

The following year, Jeffries gave a rare insight into the constraints he was under at a parliamentary hearing into the Juukan Gorge disaster, when Rio Tinto infamously blew up the ancient caves in the Pilbara. In his evidence, Jeffries spoke candidly about negotiating with the companies on the Burrup, saying he wanted it put on notice, "as I stand here today and speak openly and honestly about our experience in consulting and negotiating with major industry proponents, that there is a real fear, a genuine fear, that there will be financial repercussions for MAC if I do so."

Jeffries did not go into detail. He was not naive. Before becoming MAC's chief executive, he had worked for both Woodside and Rio. He knew how things were. Ever since Woodside built its first gas plant on the Burrup, each wave of industrial development unleashed opposition from local Indigenous groups, archaeologists and environmentalists, united by the threat posed to Murujuga's extraordinary cultural heritage. Over two decades, the companies, backed by state and federal governments, have learnt to navigate that opposition and keep building.

*

Back in 2003, the five Indigenous groups – Ngarluma, Yindjibarndi, Yaburara, Mardudhunera and Wong-Goo-Tt-Oo – that now make up MAC had native title claims over the Burrup Peninsula. These were destined to fail in the courts because the Flying Foam Massacre had broken continual occupation of the land. When the WA government threatened to compulsorily acquire the land, the Indigenous groups relinquished their claims in a deal dubbed the Burrup and Maitland Industrial Estates Agreement, which recognised them as the Traditional Custodians of Murujuga and provided some financial support from the companies and government. MAC was set up to represent them.

The WA government secured over half the Burrup Peninsula for continued industrial purposes. Eventually MAC got freehold title to most of the remaining area, which became the Murujuga National Park. Under the agreement, MAC could raise concerns over heritage sites under threat and negotiate to protect them, but it was limited by a clause in the agreement that it could not lodge objections to developments on the industrial lands. A critical legacy of the agreement was a state government commitment to a rock art monitoring program to examine whether the companies' pollution posed a threat to the petroglyphs. As one negotiator put it to me, one of the central issues at that time was how to protect the rock art – and that remains so today.

In 2022, Professor Ben Smith co-authored an explosive paper on industrial pollution on the Burrup and its effect on rock art. The paper reviewed research on whether the patina surface, or crust, on the rocks on Murujuga could dissolve under certain acidic conditions caused by industrial emissions and whether this could accelerate the rocks' natural rates of weathering – degrading the colour contrast of the petroglyphs so much that over time the images could disappear. Smith and his co-authors concluded that yes, the industrial emissions posed "a constant threat to the integrity and survival of the rock art." Smith argues Woodside is already violating government approvals to operate because of its industrial emissions. "That is why this is such a contentious issue," he told me. "In Woodside's licence to operate, it says that they may only continue to operate so long as they operate in a manner that doesn't damage the rock art. It's very clear that they're in breach of that. And that's why there is this denial going back and forth."

Woodside and the other Burrup companies dismissed Smith's 2022 paper, saying it was at odds with many years of both state government and company-sponsored research. Meg O'Neill publicly rejected it at the Woodside AGM that year. The critics also pointed out one of Smith's co-authors, Dr John Black, was a member of FARA, Friends of Australian Rock Art, who had long sought to discredit previous WA government rock art monitoring done by the CSIRO.

Despite this pushback, Smith and Black's research paper dropped at a difficult time for Woodside and Perdaman, which was what the authors intended. The final state and federal government approvals for their developments hung in the balance. The previous September, in advice to government, the state EPA gave the Perdaman plant a tick but stipulated that it must "ensure that no air emissions from the proposal have an adverse impact accelerating the weathering of rock art within Murujuga beyond natural rates." The EPA advice on Woodside's NWS extension included the same condition in June 2022. As a precaution, the EPA endorsed a compromise, suggested by Woodside, that the plant's key industrial emissions should be reduced at least 40 per cent by 2030.

Adding to the companies' worries, that June, Tanya Plibersek had been appointed the new federal environment minister and her responsibilities included Aboriginal heritage protection laws. The Save Our Songlines rebels, led by Raelene Cooper and Josie Alec, were determined to pressure Plibersek to block the new developments. With help from a group of the climate activists and rock art specialists, they filed an emergency application to halt work on the Perdaman site. The SOS application zeroed in on the two vexed issues in Perdaman's plans: industrial emissions and the threatened removal of rock art from its big construction site. Even with a design aimed at minimising industrial pollution, the Perdaman plant was expected to release up to 324 tonnes of nitrogen dioxide and sulphur dioxide pollution a year – adding to the industrial emissions from Woodside's existing operations.

The fight over industrial emissions blew up in February 2025 in closed-door discussions over the World Heritage Committee's listing of Murujuga. Australia's nomination dossier stated baldly that scientific studies over twenty years "found no scientific evidence of measurable impacts from industrial emissions on the petroglyphs." The World Heritage Committee's key adviser, the International Council on Monuments and Sites (ICOMOS), challenged this and asked for access to Western Australia's Rock Art Monitoring Program second-year progress report, which the Cook government was sitting on until the state and federal elections were out of the way. Canberra handed over a copy to ICOMOS on a confidential basis.

The Australian Conservation Foundation had also sent in a submission on Murujuga to ICOMOS. While it supported the listing, it pointed out that the Albanese government was looking to approve Woodside's NWS extension to 2070, despite the plant being the single biggest source of industrial pollution currently on the Burrup. It cited Professor Ben Smith's paper as its scientific source. It called for more consultation with the local Indigenous people. After looking at all the submissions, ICOMOS baulked at endorsing Australia's nomination of Murujuga.

In a draft decision in May 2025, the World Heritage Committee described Murujuga as "an extraordinary cultural landscape of global significance," but told Canberra it had a list of recommendations from ICOMOS it wanted action on. These included the total removal of "degrading acidic emissions impacting the rock art"; stopping any further industrial development adjacent to or within Murujuga; working up a decommissioning and rehabilitation plan for the existing industrial activities already there; and finalising the work of the Murujuga Rock Art Monitoring Program.

The draft decision was an embarrassing blow for Australia, but despite this the Albanese government doubled down on support for Woodside's developments. When Albanese was swept back into power that same month, Plibersek was replaced by the straight-talking Queensland senator Murray Watt, who was poised to approve Woodside's NWS extension. Just five days before he did so, Roger Cook's government finally publicly released the second-year report of the Rock Art Monitoring Program.

The report's executive summary included two surprising findings that would help shore up Watt's decision and the World Heritage listing. It challenged scientific papers going back over a decade, including Ben Smith's, over the so-called "acid rain hypothesis" – the argument that industrial emissions on the Burrup, mixed with rainfall or heavy dew, create acids that are damaging the rock art. It also theorised that if industrial emissions had damaged the rock art, this was most likely in the past, when the old Dampier power plant used heavy fuel oil in the 1970s. The findings were leapt on by Woodside and Premier Cook. "It's very pleasing that [there is] no ongoing impact as a result of that industry activity," Cook told the media.

Ben Smith was furious. In a press conference outside state parliament, he tore up the report's executive summary, calling it a "disgrace" and "not worth the paper it is written on." While praising the "brilliant scientific work" by the fifty-odd experts on the Rock Art Monitoring Program, he accused the state government of a cover-up.

Smith's comments were dismissed by both governments, but the 800-page interim report of the Rock Art Monitoring Program was not conclusive and it was more nuanced than Cook's comments or the executive summary. The report found there was significantly "elevated porosity," which can be seen as damage to the rock surface and likely extended to the subsurface of engraved rocks. This damage was found on rocks centred around the Dampier port and in the main industrial precinct, where Woodside and the other plants operate. But after eighteen months of monitoring the report found that current rainfall on the Burrup was more neutral or alkaline than acidic and so were the collected sample dust deposits. The question then was: if the damage to the rocks wasn't triggered by an "acid rain" effect, was there another way industrial emissions could damage the rock art? The answer in the lengthy report was – possibly, yes.

In their lab experiments, the Curtin scientists found that when they exposed sample rocks from the Burrup to high levels of nitrogen dioxide (NO_2), sulphur dioxide (SO_2) and ammonia – the key industrial emissions on the Burrup – they did indeed see damage similar to that on rocks near the Dampier port and Woodside's plants. "Overall, it appears that some anthropogenic impacts have occurred," the report concluded, most likely when emissions levels were higher than today. But it added a caveat: "The likely dominant mechanism for any effect appears to be direct impact of emissions rather than rainfall which is not currently acidic as previous research has suggested." It called for further investigation to test this hypothesis.

When I spoke to the lead researcher of the report, Professor Ben Mullins, he said the science was complicated. "We've demonstrated that it's possible for high levels of those gases, NO_2, SO_2 and ammonia, to chemically react directly with the more sensitive components of the rock to create that weathering." What may be happening, he explained, is "an interaction between the microbes, the rock and one or more air pollutants," causing an acidic defence response. But this has yet to be confirmed. It is also possible the microbes could react like this regardless of the emissions, he said.

More controversially, Mullins said the report showed that industrial emissions and air pollution were worse in the past, and if the earlier scientific papers on historic "acid rain" measurements were believed, then it's likely the damage found on the rocks may not be ongoing. But this is not definitive and it's a vital question because the key job of the Rock Art Monitoring Program is to set the criteria for a safe level of industrial emissions on the Burrup today which will protect the petroglyphs. Some of the program's own readings near the Karratha gas plant found levels of NO_2 that crossed their first threshold of warning. "So, is that a bit of a red flag for you?" I asked. Mullins pointed out these particular readings were incomplete, only taken over six months, but he did say, "I think obviously the levels need to be monitored, and would ideally stay below those levels."

When I asked the bottom-line question – does the report say there is no impact on the rock art from today's industrial emissions? – Mullins gave a cautious scientific response. "It's always very difficult to say there's absolutely no impact. On the balance of probability, it's much more likely that any impact has been in the past, and the current levels that we're seeing in the last couple of years are not having an impact, but there obviously remains some ongoing question. So we can't be absolutely definitive on that."

In other words, the Rock Art Monitoring Program needs more data and its work needs more time. Meanwhile, Professor Ben Smith and his colleague Dr John Black remain convinced the damage from current emissions is ongoing, pointing out that industrial pollution on the Burrup remains high today.

The uncertainties in the Rock Art Monitoring Program report did not stop Murray Watt approving Woodside's NWS extension days after it was released. The battle between Australia's environment movement and Woodside hit a rancorous climax and the World Heritage listing for Murujuga looked like it might become collateral damage in that battle. Watt's approval came with conditions on Woodside that are yet to be made public, but he said in a statement: "I have ensured that adequate protection of the rock art is central to my proposed decision."

*

In the furore over the industrial emissions, the bigger picture on Murujuga was lost on the media but not on the World Heritage Committee's adviser, ICOMOS. Its March report stressed that the proximity of big industrial developments to the cultural landscape of Murujuga "constitutes a threat to its integrity."

Back in 2022 Plibersek had rejected the emergency application by Josie Alec and Raelene Cooper from Save Our Songlines to stop work on the site of the giant Perdaman fertiliser plant after she visited the Burrup and spoke with both MAC's leaders and the Perdaman team. Dismissing SOS, she recognised MAC and its Circle of Elders as the most representative organisation on cultural knowledge, saying they had agreed to the removal of some rock art. She was, as she put it, "as confident as I can be that everybody is taking the incredible history of the region seriously and taking the safety of these artifacts seriously."

But Plibersek must have known members of MAC's Circle of Elders were distressed about Perdaman's construction plans, especially about the relocation of several pieces of rock art from the site. MAC CEO Peter Jeffries spelt this out clearly in a frank nine-page letter he wrote to her department. Jeffries pointed out that the Circle of Elders had refused permission to relocate any rock art from the site multiple times before finally agreeing while noting the power imbalance between Aboriginal corporations and industry. "The Circle of Elders have made it clear on numerous occasions that their preference is for rock art to remain in situ and undisturbed," he wrote. "[Perdaman] has advised on numerous occasions that this was not possible and Circle of Elders have made their recommendation to relocate these sites on that basis."

Josie Alec was disappointed but unsurprised by Plibersek's decision. By then Alec had gone to work for the ACF and had seen Plibersek in action. "I believe she had no choice but to approve it," she told me. "I admire her for being a woman in that job, but she can't change anything. She walks in two worlds. If she doesn't sign off on it, she's in trouble with her mob."

Heather Builth, a prominent heritage consultant, was hired by MAC in 2021 after she famously blew the whistle on the Juukan Gorge explosion. Jeffries asked her to help with the heritage survey for the government infrastructure to support the plant. She soon became alarmed by the impact the Perdaman plant would have, not only on the site but also on the surrounding area.

"It wasn't just four or five areas. It was a landscape, it was a waterscape, it was the Country. They didn't realise how much it was going to be affected by this Perdaman build," she said. "That's what I got frustrated and upset about, because they don't realise what's going to happen."

Builth felt there was little anyone could do to change the outcome. "It was like a card game deal," she said. At the end of her contract, she left MAC dismayed. She later sent me aerial photographs of the large bulldozed Perdaman site straddling both sides of the road that locals and tourists take to the Deep Gorge trail. "It's heartbreaking," she said. "It's more than just the relocation of three engraved rocks, a million times more than that."

One of the most respected members of MAC's Circle of Elders, Tootsie Daniel, known as "the Queen of Roebourne," spoke out against the developments shortly before her death in November 2024. She recorded a message calling on Plibersek to protect Murujuga: "Where is Tanya going to be in fifty years? She could be cast away on a ship or something and go somewhere else. But we always there, and that's our home. Burrup is a place that should be looked after and cared for, not for industry to go there."

Many of MAC's members want employment and training for their children and grandchildren and some are hoping the new Burrup developments will provide this. But the economic benefit the Traditional Custodians get from the $6-billion Perdaman plant will be a tiny fraction of its value. Most of the 2500 jobs touted in Perdaman's press releases are in the construction phase of the plant. The small print reveals that, once it's built, only around 200 operational jobs will be required.

For MAC's leaders, its heritage team and the Albanese government, when the World Heritage Committee baulked at listing Murujuga it was a profound shock. Murray Watt blamed the environment movement for the setback and was also highly critical of ICOMOS, telling *The West Australian*, "Some of the conditions requested by the subcommittee were unreasonable and unrealistic, in the sense that they call for the total decommissioning of current industry there as well, when there is no scientific evidence to support the conclusion that the current industry is a threat to the rock art."

In the weeks before the July UNESCO meeting to hear the nomination bid, Watt mobilised a major diplomatic lobbying effort to swing around the World Heritage Committee delegates. By the time MAC's leadership, including Peter Hicks and former CEO Peter Jeffries, along with their heritage advisers and the leader of the Rock Art Monitoring Program, Professor Ben Mullins, arrived in Paris with Watt, they faced a string of meetings to persuade the delegates that the rock art is being protected, the original ICOMOS advice was overreach and they should back the listing. Their huge effort paid off. When the gavel fell announcing Murujuga's inscription on the World Heritage List, the Australian delegation with MAC's leaders cheered from the floor. Some shed tears. Decades of work had gone into achieving the listing. The Murujuga petroglyphs were recognised as "a manifestation of creative genius inscribed in the landscape since deep time." Watching on from the sidelines were Raelene Cooper, Piers Verstegen and Jesse Noakes.

The fraught issue of industrial emissions on the Burrup has not gone away. The listing will place far greater obligations on both state and federal governments to ensure the vital scientific work monitoring the emissions continues and the final results can demonstrate convincingly that the rock art is being protected.

No doubt the success in Paris will convince Woodside and the Albanese government that the extraordinary ancient rock art and Murujuga's cultural heritage can coexist with industry on the Burrup. That Australia can have its cake and eat it too. But for a visitor admiring the celebrated petroglyphs at Deep Gorge in the Murujuga National Park, it is impossible not to wonder why, in 2025, a giant new fertiliser plant, fed by fossil fuels, emitting large amounts of greenhouse gases along with industrial pollution, is being built within a kilometre's walk of this manifestation of human creative genius.

For anyone closely following Canberra politics, the Albanese government's approval of Woodside's NWS extension straight after the federal election was pretty much a given. A year earlier, in May 2024, Madeleine King, the federal resources minister, had released the government's *Future Gas Strategy* and one of its six guiding principles was that Australia "is and will remain" a reliable trading partner for energy, including LNG exports. Unveiling the strategy, King echoed the words of Roger Cook and Meg O'Neill: our trading partners are relying on Australian gas to transition their economies to net zero.

The gas strategy shocked the climate movement, teal MPs and even some Labor backbenchers, because it appeared to lock Australia into major gas production and exports for decades to come. The Climate Council's Dr Jennifer Rayner called it an echo of the past: "Now is not the moment to add to our climate crisis by burning more gas. Signing Australia up to a future made on gas ignores climate scientists, who warn we are at risk of smashing through 1.5°C of warming." The Smart Energy Council's chief executive, John Grimes, trashed it: "The gas lobby's power over governments of all persuasions is on full display here, and it's a horror show. This is Woodside's blueprint for the future, it can't be the Australian Government's blueprint for the future."

The climate movement saw a contradiction at the heart of the *Future Gas Strategy*. Its stated intention was to set a pathway for Australia to be both "a trusted gas producer" and "a responsible climate actor," but the two aims were hard to reconcile. Instead, it read as if Australia's role of gas producer – both at home and in Asia – was the priority, and this was welcomed by the gas industry.

In 2022, when Albanese first won government, the Russian invasion of Ukraine triggered a global energy crisis, sending Australian gas prices skyrocketing, energy bills soaring and manufacturers screaming over the lack of affordable supply. Ministers scrambled to contain the crisis, including resorting to an emergency order to cap gas prices for a year. That provoked a fierce backlash from the gas industry, both foreign and local, with Santos's chief executive, Kevin Gallagher, declaring, "This Soviet-style policy is a form of nationalisation." Tensions and prices had eased only a little by 2023, when the government set up a mandatory code designed to ensure domestic gas at reasonable prices. This included using the Turnbull-era domestic gas security mechanism as a measure of last resort to limit exports and ensure adequate local supply. In negotiations with the industry, the government promised gas producers "the certainty they need to invest in supply, and ensure LNG producers meet their export commitments." The *Future Gas Strategy* was released a year later. While its first guiding principle was a commitment to net zero by 2050, its second was gas affordability and its third was support for more gas developments.

Madeleine King's seat of Brand covers Perth's sprawling southern suburbs, including the industrial city of Kwinana, not far from where she grew up and where her father once worked at the local BP refinery. Her mentor was Gary Gray, the legendary Labor Party federal secretary who went on to work for Woodside as a senior executive before he was elected as the MP for Brand. Gray hired King as an adviser when he was a minister in the Gillard government and backed her to take the seat when he retired. King's critics, like Carmen Lawrence, accuse her of gas industry boosterism. "As a minister, she's the decision-maker, she's not an advocate," Lawence complained.

I asked King for her response to the climate scientists and activists who say no new gas developments should go ahead if the world wants to get to net zero by 2050 and she dismissed the idea out of hand. "Well, that's just economically unviable," she said bluntly. "The 'no new gas' or 'no new coal' is about as unhelpful as the 'drill, baby, drill' stuff. It's just not helpful because it's not real." King's firm view is that no new gas developments would mean asking Australians to change their way of life. "We're aiming for net zero by 2050, as many other economies are, and we're determined to get there, as they are. How we get there is a very big challenge. There's no doubt about it."

King is right about the size of the challenge. The *Future Gas Strategy* says that Australia can't reach net zero by 2050 without both sharply cutting its gas use and decarbonising where possible. The same thing, of course, holds for our gas customers overseas. If Japan and South Korea are going to decarbonise and get to net zero by 2050, their gas imports from Australia could start falling steeply by the early 2030s.

This possibility is buried in the *Future Gas Strategy*. One of its more confronting graphs looks at three scenarios for Australia's LNG exports out to 2050. The first scenario (net-zero emissions) aligns with 1.5°C of warming, where our LNG exports fall 90 per cent by 2050. The second scenario aligns with 1.8°C of warming, where they fall 75 per cent by 2050. This scenario is based on existing climate targets promised by world governments being delivered in full, with no increased ambition.

Only in the final scenario, one aligned with 2.6°C of warming, do our LNG exports hold up, falling just 19 per cent by 2050. That scenario was based on the Stated Policies Scenario (STEPS) – the global climate and energy policies being followed, which had the world on course for warming of up to 2.6°C by 2100. According to the UN, this could even extend to 3°C, with the planet facing mass extinctions, big falls in food production and major disruptions to water supplies caused by the rapid melting of half the world's glaciers.

Woodside commissions its own consultants and O'Neill professed to have little doubt from their modelling that Woodside's LNG exports will hold up well. "We're very confident in sustained demand for LNG in the decades to come. When we look at our projects, our projects are cost-competitive, but we also see strong demand from our customers," she said, pointing to long-term contracts signed last year for the Scarborough project. "Asia is a key driver … Vietnam, the Philippines, for example, recently imported LNG for the first time in the last two years. We're having discussions with Cambodia, who are trying to explore LNG imports to meet their long-term energy needs. So we're very confident in the demand for LNG over the long run."

O'Neill is bullish, but given the fall in global LNG demand required to keep global warming in check, it's becoming increasingly difficult for the gas industry and the Albanese government to keep avoiding the critical question: how much Australian LNG is actually going to *help* Asian countries decarbonise in the next two decades, and how much will *hinder* them? The International Energy Agency's 2024 World Energy Outlook report canvassed a scenario where global gas demand did keep growing out to the 2030s and beyond. But it found this depended in part on a slow-down in the take-up of clean energy, stalling energy efficiency, and LNG prices so low that exporters would struggle to recover their costs. The IEA warned, "Decisions by governments, investors and consumers still too often entrench the flaws in today's energy system, rather than pushing it towards a cleaner and safer path."

In March 2025, the federal industry department's own resource and energy figures predicted Australia's LNG export revenue will fall heavily in the next five years, from $72 billion to just $45 billion by 2029–30, partly because of falling prices. Demand from our key customer, Japan, is also expected to fall. LNG imports to Japan peaked some years ago and Japanese energy companies regularly on-sell Australian gas to other countries. This might shock many Australians, who hear politicians carry on about energy-hungry Japan's need for gas and coal. Japan does rely on Australian gas to power its cities, but since the Paris Agreement Japan has also become a major gas trader in its own right, investing in gas developments in Asia, America and the Middle East and building its own gas empire, in which Australia is just one player.

An investigation by Bloomberg reporters in 2024 found Japan's gas business is now so big that every six hours, somewhere in the world, a shipment of LNG controlled by a Japanese company leaves a port. Not only does Japan own the world's largest fleet of LNG tankers, but one of its leading companies, Mitsubishi Heavy Industries, is one of the world's biggest suppliers of gas turbines. The Japanese government actively pushes both LNG and gas technology financed by Japanese banks to countries using the same message as Australia: gas will help nations decarbonise during the energy transition.

Madeleine King won't comment on specific reports that Japan is reselling Australian LNG, but she knows the role Japan plays as a global gas trader and supports it. "When they on-sell, what they are providing is that regional energy security, whether that be to Vietnam, I think Taiwan has been mentioned in some reports, [and] perhaps the Philippines," she told me. "I mean, it is a good thing that those countries have energy security. Regional energy security is of extraordinarily vital importance to our national interest, because it delivers regional stability and it delivers regional prosperity. And that is what we want for this region."

For decades Japan's energy policy has been central to Australia's trade and foreign policy and its climate policy. Deep in the DNA of most Australian politicians is the belief that relations with our second-most important trading partner must survive and thrive through the energy transition. We sell Japan our iron ore, coal and gas; it sells us back cars, trucks and diesel to run them. But after Albanese's election in 2022, tensions surfaced over Labor's promise for stronger action on climate change. Japan quickly made it clear it stood on the side of the Australian gas lobby. High-profile Japanese energy executives and even the outgoing Japanese ambassador accused the Albanese government of undermining confidence in the Australian LNG industry. In an extraordinary intervention, reported in *The Australian Financial Review*, Takayuki Ueda, the head of Inpex, Japan's oil and gas giant, used a Parliament House function hosted by King to criticise Australia for what he called its "quiet quitting" of the LNG business. He warned this had "potentially very sinister consequences" as it opened the way for China, Russia and Iran to fill the global energy void. Japanese gas investors supported the Australian gas lobby's campaign to use international carbon offsets to cover emissions; its call for more government support for carbon capture and storage; cuts to approval times for projects; and curbs on Canberra's power to secure gas for the domestic market. Japan itself remains one of the world's top-ten greenhouse gas emitters and has been slow to ramp up its own use of renewable energy. When it recently announced new climate targets for 2035, pledging a 60 per cent decline on 2013 emissions, it was criticised by the climate movement at home and abroad for lacking the ambition expected from a world-leading industrial power.

*

Chris Bowen, the climate and energy minister, likes to say the hardest things he's ever done in politics are his two signature climate-change policies: reforming the Safeguard Mechanism to reduce greenhouse gas emissions from big polluting industries like Woodside; and bringing in new vehicle efficiency standards to cut transport emissions. Both were ferociously opposed by the Coalition. "Both were hard-fought, [with] vested interests railing against them declaring the end of Western civilisation," he told me. "Both of them have critics who say they haven't gone far enough. Well, we've got them done and they both could have easily fallen apart."

When climate activists attack the government for approving "carbon bombs" like Scarborough and the NWS extension, Bowen says that the Safeguard Mechanism is cutting emissions at Australia's big LNG operations.

Given the heated debates over the Safeguard Mechanism, it's worth looking briefly at what it does and doesn't do. It covers 219 big facilities around the country which emit more than 100,000 tonnes of greenhouse gases a year. These include not only LNG plants but coalmines, cement factories, waste disposal sites, steel mills, aluminium refineries, coal generators and gasfields. The plants, on average, have to reduce their emissions from a set baseline by 4.9 per cent every year until 2030, in line with Australia's national emissions target. After that, their emissions will decline steadily to reach net zero by 2050. The operators can reduce their emissions with energy efficiency redesigns or using onsite renewable energy, but if they can't do this, they can use carbon credits – from schemes such as forest regeneration – to offset their emissions. The carbon credits used by many big companies are called Australian Carbon Credit Units (ACCUs) and currently sell on the spot market for about $35 to cover a tonne of greenhouse gas emissions.

Close to a third of all Australia's emissions are regulated by the Safeguard Mechanism, so it's a big deal. While it's not a carbon price, it's often been called a de facto one and Bowen strongly defends it. "If I had brought down a carbon price and said you've got these big polluters who've got to pay $35 a tonne for anything they emit, many people would say, 'Oh, that's wonderful. He's taken on the big reform.'" Bowen argues the Safeguard Mechanism is "more effective than a carbon price" because it puts pressure on company boards to reduce emissions rather than pay for more offsets.

The policy is designed to work with the government's ambitious targets of 82 per cent renewable energy by 2030 and net-zero emissions by 2050 (under the Paris Agreement) to force down Australia's use of fossil fuels. Critics of the Safeguard Mechanism say it undermines Australia's climate ambition because companies like Woodside use too many offsets and avoid real emissions cuts at their operations. According to the Australia Institute's Ketan Joshi, the North West Shelf project operated by Woodside met 100 per cent of excess emissions last year by using carbon offsets. The figures are confirmed by data on the Clean Energy Regulator's website.

O'Neill insisted Woodside aims to "design out" and "operate out" to reduce its plants' emissions, but said it still needs to use offsets where it can't do this. "Those offsets are all subject to rigorous quality checks to ensure that if we are claiming that we've removed CO_2 from the atmosphere, we genuinely have. I'll go back to the science. You look at the IPCC reports, they're very clear that carbon dioxide removal absolutely needs to be part of the world solution to tackle on climate change."

Bowen also defends offsets as vital to getting business support for the Safeguard Mechanism. He reminds critics the policy is in its early days and needs time to work. He also reminds them he has repeatedly pushed back on heavy lobbying from the big polluters to use international offsets, which he believes have serious credibility problems. But Bowen is feeling the heat from a barrage of potent attacks, led by the Australia Institute, on the credibility of the local offset schemes and their liberal use by big emitters. The Australasian Centre for Corporate Responsibility also makes the point that few countries in the world with national carbon-pricing schemes allow more than a 10 per cent use of offsets by big polluters.

Bowen is promising offsets will be on the table when a review of the Safeguard Mechanism takes place next year. Whatever changes come out of that review, they won't address the core problem for many in the climate movement: the Safeguard Mechanism only covers Scope 1 emissions, produced onsite in Australia, and does nothing to cut Scope 3 emissions, from eventual use of the gas. Under the UN's climate treaties, it was assumed customer countries are responsible for those emissions and this has always advantaged fossil-fuel-exporting countries like Australia. Climate campaigners argue this is no longer acceptable.

For Piers Verstegen, it goes to the heart of the matter. "Under the Albanese government, to make the 2030 targets that have been set, we need to reduce Australia's emissions by about 950 million tonnes of CO_2," he explains. "But the fossil-fuel projects that are being approved and supported under the government are going to release more than seven times that. And that's always been the elephant in the room in Australia's climate policy and it's not one that can be addressed by saying, 'Well, we're going to leave it to the market.'"

The battle against Burrup Hub is where Verstegen and his colleagues in the west decided to draw the line. "I see it as a West Australian," he says. "We should be taking responsibility for the impact of what happens here. It's our government. We elect it. It's our gas. It's been extracted out of Western Australia and that CO_2 will be in the atmosphere and have an impact even if it goes by China or India or one of these other places."

*

The Burrup Hub campaign took on national significance because it is an existential challenge to Australia's status as both a trusted gas producer and a responsible climate actor. For Albanese, maintaining this balancing act is a political priority, especially in Western Australia. But this is not about the lights going out in Perth when Western Australia shuts down its coal generators in 2030; it's about the state's industrial future. It's about making fertilisers, explosives, extracting and processing minerals, including critical minerals for the energy transition. When Albanese talks about the Future Made in Australia fund, he talks about green hydrogen, decarbonising steel and renewable energy, but in Western Australia they talk about gas, and how these industries will depend on it, possibly for decades to come.

"The biggest increase in the use of gas on the west coast is around minerals processing," Madeleine King told me. "So that's what it is right now, and it will be for the foreseeable future. Companies themselves will look to alternatives if they can find them, but right now it's gas that will be required for that minerals processing, and we need that minerals processing so that we can build the green energy technology that we want to have in place in Australia and elsewhere to reduce emissions."

Meg O'Neill sees it the same way as King. "If you look at the *Future Gas Strategy*, it's very clear in that document that the Labor government backs the need for gas in Australia and Australian gas in our region to 2050, and beyond. That's meeting current industrial demands, but also contributing … to things like critical minerals processing," she told me. "Those sorts of manufacturing and processing facilities need 24/7 reliable power. Renewables will be part of that mix, but you've got to have something to provide that firming power to ensure that the plants can run reliably, and gas is going to be the natural outcome."

King pointed out that companies opening new critical minerals projects will come under the Safeguard Mechanism if their emissions are high, but when I asked whether it was justifiable to launch big new projects that are so dependent on gas, she was adamant it was. "Well, if we don't start these minerals-processing industries, we won't have the things we need for a secure future," she said. She listed electric vehicles, battery storage and photovoltaic cells needed for green energy. "There's no option around not having a critical minerals–processing industry in this country. We are going to do it, and we should do it, and I'm determined to do it."

But it's worth noting that some of these companies are looking at greener energy for future production. One of Western Australia's most successful critical minerals operations, Lynas Rare Earths, already has plans to cut emissions by moving from diesel generation to a hybrid power station at its Mount Weld mine. Lynas hired Zenith Energy, a specialist in remote power for miners, to design a power plant using wind, solar and batteries with a back-up gas station and standby diesel generation. This is still the exception rather than the rule, and the Cook government is constantly ringing alarm bells about the crisis facing WA industry and blue-collar jobs unless new gas projects like Woodside's go ahead.

This crisis atmosphere over gas shortages helped drive a dramatic policy shift by the Cook government in 2024, aimed at speeding up project approvals. Cook argued this was to support big new renewable projects as well as the gas projects. But the changes limit the rights of activists to challenge gas and resource projects and, importantly, limit the role of the WA EPA advising on greenhouse gas emissions. Five years after Woodside first went to war with the state EPA over greenhouse gas emissions, Cook made clear that any plant or facility in Western Australia covered by the Safeguard Mechanism should not have their emissions regulated by the state. Cook declared this "strikes the right balance – slashing green tape, removing duplication, and reducing delays – all while maintaining the highest environmental standards." O'Neill praised his decision, telling me, "I would commend the Cook government for simplifying and getting to a place where one body, which is the federal agencies through the Safeguard Mechanism, regulates industrial projects with significant emissions. So great for WA."

Cook's campaign of "slashing green tape" left Tanya Plibersek's attempts to overhaul the federal environment laws in 2024 dead in the water. Her long-promised Nature Positive laws ran into heavy opposition from the WA Chamber of Minerals and Energy over demands from the Greens, the ACF and others in the environment movement to include a "climate trigger" in them. This, along with business fears about the powers of an independent environmental watchdog – a federal EPA – unleashed a brutal campaign in Western Australia against Plibersek and the new laws.

The Nature Positive laws were supposed to overhaul Australia's failed federal environment laws following Professor Graeme Samuel's review of the

EPBC Act. That review called for legally enforceable national environment standards and new oversight bodies to monitor and enforce those standards in an effort to turn around Australia's woeful record of species extinction. The Samuel review didn't support a "climate trigger" to force big greenhouse gas–emitting projects to be assessed under the *EPBC Act*, saying it shouldn't duplicate federal laws like the Safeguard Mechanism. But in a critical change, it did say big projects should disclose their greenhouse gas emissions in full and standards should be set to consider the effectiveness of their plans to cut emissions if the projects have a significant environmental impact.

Cook became one of most vocal and influential opponents of the Nature Positive laws. As his spokesman put it, "We will support reforms that achieve the dual objectives of delivering faster approvals and strengthening environmental protection. What we won't support is any measure that will cost jobs by making Western Australia a less attractive place for industry to invest." Meg O'Neill told me Woodside wanted a federal approvals process that was not "vulnerable to manipulation by activist groups whose only desire is to stop projects proceeding."

During her term as environment minister, Plibersek compromised several times on the reforms, splitting them up and limiting the proposed powers of a federal EPA after relentless media attacks from Kerry Stokes' Seven West group. With both Cook and Albanese facing elections in early 2025, Stokes' influence in WA was at its peak. The Nature Positive laws looked friendless, without support from either the Greens or the Opposition, when Stokes hosted his annual Seven West Telethon Ball in October 2024. Among the prominent guests were Albanese and Opposition leader Peter Dutton and their partners, along with Roger Cook. *The West Australian* posted happy snaps of Albanese and fiancée Jodie Haydon with Meg O'Neill and Richard Goyder.

In the dying weeks of the 2024 parliamentary session, Plibersek made a stab at rescuing Nature Positive after the Greens offered to drop their demand for a climate trigger. With the support of the Greens and Senator David Pocock, Plibersek thought Labor had a chance to get the laws through the Senate. So did the Greens' environment spokesperson, Sarah Hanson-Young, until last-minute lobbying from Western Australia sank the deal. During the final day of negotiations, Hanson-Young said, she heard from government sources that "Roger Cook is on the warpath" and that the mining lobby was in full swing trying to stop the legislation. When she and Greens leader Adam Bandt met with Albanese and Labor's Senate leader, Katy Gallagher, to go through the Senate legislative list, they got to the Nature Positive laws and Albanese baulked. "No. Can't do it," was the message. "I knew right there and then that it was dead," said Hanson-Young.

Plibersek was still working on amendments when Hanson-Young texted her with the news. "I had to say the prime minister has killed it," she told me. Albanese later argued Labor didn't have the numbers in the Senate, but Hanson-Young said she was in no doubt Cook's lobbying was decisive. "It was only a matter of hours before Roger Cook was standing up at the event in Perth claiming victory – that he had, you know, got this killed off. I didn't have to tell anybody what had happened. It was all over the front pages of the newspapers." Cook more or less confirmed this to the local media, saying, "We are of the view that Nature Positive posed a risk to our mining industry and a risk to the nation's prosperity. We put that view very firmly to the federal government."

By the end of Albanese's first term in office, the gas companies and the Labor governments in WA and Canberra had refined their defence of the LNG industry in the face of the far-reaching campaign by activists to challenge Woodside's social licence. But the narrative was the same as it had been a decade ago: the gas industry was helping the world decarbonise, curbing its emissions through buying offsets, supporting the energy transition and providing energy security. It sounded like the planet could hardly have a better friend than Australia's LNG industry and companies like Woodside.

The ditching of the Nature Positive laws was just one more breach in relations between Labor and the climate movement during the long, fraught battle over the Burrup Hub, and Cook and Albanese were more than willing to wear the consequences. Both leaders were re-elected with thumping majorities. As their supporters celebrated, Labor could argue its strategy of steering a course through the energy transition as a trusted gas producer for Asia and a responsible climate actor was a winning one. That is, of course, if you were seeing it through eyes of a political pundit.

Through the eyes of a climate scientist, the strategy clearly has its limits. Just days before Albanese called the 2025 election, the World Meteorological Organization's annual *State of the Global Climate* report was released. Once again, the year just past was the hottest on record, 1.55°C above pre-industrial levels. Once again, the oceans were the hottest on record, with rising levels of acidification. And once again, greenhouse gases continued to rise, passing levels not seen for 800,000 years. The planet was still heading for a perilous future as responsible climate actors continued to export fossil fuels.

A couple of days after Meg O'Neill was blasted by whistleblowing activists at Woodside's AGM, she jetted out of Perth for a much warmer welcome in Riyadh, joining a global corporate elite on stage at the Saudi–US Investment Forum with US president Donald Trump and Saudi Arabia's Crown Prince Mohammed bin Salman. The forum was showcasing US$600 billion in promised Saudi investment in the United States, helping to "make America great again." In the White House press briefing, just one of the deals mentioned named an Australian company: Woodside. The Saudi national oil company, Aramco, was exploring investing in Woodside's big new LNG plant, not on the Burrup Hub but in Calcasieu Parish in the US state of Louisiana.

Signing the agreement with Aramco, O'Neill said it was part of Woodside's strategic vision to build "a diverse and resilient global portfolio." Just weeks earlier Woodside had finalised its plans for the three-train Louisiana LNG plant with other big investors, part of an ambition to become a global LNG powerhouse exporting across the Atlantic and Pacific and capturing 5 per cent of the world LNG supply by the 2030s. O'Neill left no doubt Woodside is doubling down on its bet that LNG will be the transition fuel for decades to come.

Woodside's prospective partners are also bullish on LNG, especially since Trump's election. Aramco's CEO, Amin Nasser, told a world energy conference in March 2025 that investment in all forms of energy, not just renewables, had to grow in the transition. "Certainly, that includes new and alternative energy sources. But they will complement conventional energy, not replace it in any meaningful way."

This is the new "energy realism" narrative being pushed by Trump's White House: as energy demand grows, especially with the advance of AI, affordable and reliable energy is dependent on big new investments in fossil fuels like LNG, regardless of renewables. When Trump was re-elected and pulled America out of the Paris Agreement, the energy realism narrative was embraced by international bankers, global asset managers and US hedge fund investors, who joined a stampede to dump their pledges to the net-zero banking alliance which has promised to finance an energy transition aligned to the Paris goals.

In Australia, O'Neill still portrays Woodside's new investments in LNG as the way to reduce greenhouse gas emissions in Asia while ensuring affordability and reliability in the energy transition. The big question for Woodside is whether its shareholders will continue to buy the narrative if voters demand a faster energy transition as the impacts of climate change ratchet up and the cost of renewables keeps going down. In that case, LNG demand will likely begin to fall sooner rather than later, hitting Woodside's investments on the Burrup Hub and in Louisiana. For Australians like me, with a superannuation fund heavily invested in Woodside, that will focus our attention. This self-interested financial fear is what shareholder activists are relying on to pressure Woodside's big investors to change the company's direction. Right now, O'Neill is confident she is winning the argument that gas is a great investment for the future. "Our strategy is very much focused on thriving through the energy transition. If you contrast it with [those of our] peers, we've not walked back or changed any of our ambitions," she told me. "I think our gas-focused strategy really does demonstrate how we can deliver on all those goals – lower emissions intensity than coal, so a natural partner to renewables – again, to try to lower emissions even further but also providing economic security and underpinning prosperity both in Australia and abroad."

Alex Hillman, the former Woodside climate adviser turned shareholder activist, doesn't buy it. In his work for the Australasian Centre for Corporate Responsibility, he crunches the numbers for gas investments and energy scenarios. He believes Woodside is greatly overestimating the long-term demand for its LNG. "They've got a business they want to run, and they tell a story to justify it, which is around gas helping to displace coal and support renewables. I think both of those things, displacing coal and supporting renewables, are dramatically overblown." In a radical suggestion for most Australian politicians, Hillman said Woodside needs to think about shrinking its gas business, not expanding it. "We think it's a pretty compelling financial case that Woodside should just admit that this fossil-fuel business is going to get smaller and actually celebrate that, because it's a more valuable strategy."

Right now, this may sound farfetched, but gas companies like Woodside are under threat. Hillman argues that, globally, oil and gas businesses have made below-market returns and not come close to earning their cost of capital for the past fifteen years. "To me that makes it pretty clear that what these companies have been doing isn't working for investors."

According to the International Energy Agency, LNG exporters in Qatar and the United States have been ramping up to cash in on countries trying to reduce their emissions by replacing coal with gas. This, the IEA predicted, "is set to depress international gas prices and set the stage for fierce competition between suppliers." Unsurprisingly, O'Neill rejects this talk about oversupply: "There have been rumours of LNG gluts at multiple times in the last twenty years, none of which have ever come to pass."

Maybe so, but Woodside is being hit on two fronts. Not only is more LNG coming onto the market, but it's also facing competition from a rising tide of renewables. This year, global investment in the energy transition is set to increase twice as much as investments in oil, gas and coal. This investment is being shaped by what the IEA is calling the "Age of Electricity." The "Golden Age of Gas" that began well over a decade ago is drawing to an end.

China was the world's biggest LNG importer and Australia's second-biggest LNG customer in 2023. But China's prospects as a long-term lucrative coal-to-gas switching customer are in doubt. Instead, its massive investment in renewable energy is disrupting fossil-fuel markets around the world. You can get a striking insight into the scale of China's renewables revolution by looking at satellite images from NASA's Earth Observatory of the "Solar Great Wall" in the Kubuqi Desert. The barren landscape in Inner Mongolia is now home to China's most ambitious solar project, which will help power Beijing. Adam Voiland, science writer for the NASA Earth Observatory, explained how the giant solar farm will eventually cover an area some

400 kilometres long and 5 kilometres wide when it's completed in 2030. Its capacity will be more than all of America's fifty-four commercial nuclear power plants.

China is also investing in large-scale renewables in so-called sunbelt countries – Mexico, Morocco, Egypt, Pakistan and Brazil. While Trump has abandoned a leadership role in the energy transition, China's Xi Jinping has embraced it. Today, China is the world leader in solar panel manufacturing, in onshore and offshore wind farms and in large-scale batteries. Its tech powerhouse Huawei is a global provider of smart PV technology that helps stabilise energy grids with big renewable inputs. Yes, China is still the world's biggest coal user and is still building coal-fired power stations, but its coal consumption is expected to peak in the next three years. And while there are plenty of doubters saying China won't cut its fossil-fuel use any time soon, its stunning upending of the EV market suggests otherwise. In the last five years, not only has China taken on the legacy carmakers of Japan and Europe, but its EV expansion is also beginning to affect world oil markets. As China's domestic EV sales surge, the IEA predicts its oil demand could peak by 2027.

Chris Bowen certainly gets that China is now the biggest player in the energy transition and, increasingly, the most influential. "China's investing more [in] renewables than the rest of the world combined, and that's bringing the cost curve down for all of us. The more you do something, the cheaper it gets. Now, does that mean we are over-relying on Chinese supply chains? Sure, that's why we have all sorts of policies with our Future Made in Australia. But should we recognise that China actually is making a very substantial contribution to decarbonisation, both for themselves and abroad? Yes. Could they do more? Of course, I'd love them to do more."

Bowen is pushing Australia's own ambitious 82 per cent renewable energy target by 2030 for the electricity grid in the face of trenchant opposition from the Coalition and anti-renewables groups. That target is also under pressure from rapidly rising infrastructure costs and approval delays hitting the renewables roll out. As he lobbies for Adelaide to host next year's UN climate talks, COP 31, in partnership with our Pacific neighbours, he wants to promote Australia as a green energy superpower. But Bowen also argues repeatedly that investment in new domestic gas developments is needed to back up renewables and warns climate activists that gas shortages and price hikes will undermine public support for the energy transition.

After the long battle over Burrup Hub, many in the climate movement are cynical that these arguments are being used simply to greenlight big-emitting projects. For Piers Verstegen and Dr Bill Hare, the Albanese government's decision to allow the North West Shelf plant to operate until 2070 was "a historic mistake and a denial of climate science."

The battle lines are entrenched on both sides. When I asked Meg O'Neill what lessons Woodside has learnt from the Burrup Hub campaign, her answer suggested nothing that had changed her mind. "Look, we're very attuned to the strategies and tactics of the radical environment movements. The tactics are the same as have played out in places like the US and Europe for many decades. I think we've managed it pretty well. If you look at the Scarborough energy project, for example, we have all of the approvals that we need. The project is 82 per cent complete and on track for first LNG cargo in the second half of 2026." O'Neill wanted to stick to the talking points she has honed. "I think it's important to have to recognise the complexity of what we're trying to tackle, which is a global challenge. It's a global challenge of climate change. It's a global challenge of reliable and affordable energy."

The climate movement, meanwhile, is gearing up for the next phase of the Woodside campaign: over the plans to drill in the Browse Basin. Greenpeace's David Ritter is convinced that this time the company can be stopped. "There's an opportunity for the federal minister to simply say no under the federal environmental laws," he said. "Our view is that there are very good grounds to do that on the basis of the unique environmental values of Scott Reef."

Pressed on whether Browse will go ahead, O'Neill insisted the new gasfields were needed despite concerns even in the company that the project is too costly and will have to use carbon capture and storage to bury at least some of the emissions. "Browse is challenging. Obviously, the economics are challenging. But it remains the largest discovered undeveloped gasfields in Australia's offshore and it will be incredibly important for both Western Australia's gas mix in the 2030s and 2040s, as well as to meet our customers[' demand] for LNG," she said.

The campaign over Browse will trigger a new round of legal fights, protests and drawn-out appeals. But if the battle over Burrup Hub teaches us anything, it's that Australia needs a broader, national debate about gas exports and climate change – and not the one Woodside and the gas industry want. It's one that asks: can Australia really be a responsible climate actor if it keeps developing major new gas projects as global emissions continue to rise and the chances of holding global warming to 1.5°C fade? It asks state and federal governments to assess the full impact of Australia's fossil-fuel exports on climate change both at home and abroad. It asks whether more Australian LNG exports are squeezing out the growth of renewables in our Asian neighbours.

In the past decade, Australian governments have supported Woodside and other big LNG exporters pushing new gas developments with the argument that we need more gas so the world can cut emissions from coal. While this might have been the case in the past, today this claim can no longer stand without being tested. Is there evidence new LNG exports will significantly lower global emissions, or are the gas companies vastly exaggerating? Yes, some gas will be needed to back up renewables, but how much and for how long?

The "gas is better than coal" argument sets a low bar. As the IEA points out, if you are trying to make an environmental case for continuing LNG exports, it's no longer good enough to say you are better than the most carbon-intensive fuel on the planet.

Woodside, like its peers, refuses to accept that the golden age of gas will end sooner rather than later as the climate crisis speeds up. But the climate science points in that direction. The sheer scale of emissions cuts needed to keep the temperature rise to 1.5°C is too great to keep LNG exports at levels anywhere near where they are today. Increasingly costly offsets and patchy carbon capture and storage will only make gas less competitive with renewables.

After four decades, Woodside and Australia have finally arrived in the age of accountability. Climate change and its impacts have to be reckoned with. This was brought home in July, with a landmark ruling by the International Court of Justice on the legal obligations of countries to protect the planet and its people from the threat of climate change. In a unanimous advisory opinion, the fifteen judges rejected submissions by Australia, Saudi Arabia, the US, the UK and China that argued their climate responsibility was already covered by global climate agreements, including Paris.

Instead, the court found all countries had a legal obligation under the Paris Agreement to work together to hold global warming to 1.5°C and this was not the limit of their responsibility under international law. If countries failed to meet their climate obligations, they may be held liable and open to claims for reparations over their fossil-fuel emissions. As the judges put it, "Failure of a State to take appropriate action to protect the climate system from GHG [greenhouse gas] emissions – including through fossil fuel production, fossil fuel consumption, the granting of fossil fuel exploration licences or the provision of fossil fuel subsidies – may constitute an internationally wrongful act which is attributable to that State."

While the ICJ's opinion is not legally binding, it gives guidance to courts around the world and is likely to launch a new wave of climate litigation from developing countries seeking reparations from fossil-fuel producers. Significantly, the ICJ case was initiated by Vanuatu, Australia's small Pacific neighbour on the front line of climate change.

The ICJ's findings will put pressure on the Albanese government to legislate a strong emissions reduction target for 2035 to meet its Paris obligations. That decision is supposed to happen soon. On advice from the Climate Change Authority, the target should see emissions cuts in the range of 65 to 75 per cent. The court's findings will also renew demands for a "climate trigger" in Australia's environment laws, to force big new fossil-fuel projects to be assessed on their climate impacts.

Just weeks after approving Woodside's NWS extension out to 2070, Murray Watt gathered environment leaders and business leaders for another round of talks aimed at overhauling the failed environment laws. From the outset the minister played down any chance of a climate trigger being included, using the same old arguments: we have the Safeguard Mechanism to control our emissions at home and the Paris Agreement to control our customers' emissions abroad; we don't want climate considerations to play a part in environmental approvals. The Climate Council's Amanda McKenzie disagreed, arguing it was not good enough to push climate change out of the frame. "This is the biggest impact on the Australian environment," she told *Guardian Australia*. "The law simply won't be credible if it does not consider the biggest impact on the Australian environment." Former Treasury secretary Ken Henry is also now saying a climate trigger should at least be up for discussion.

Many voters know climate change is already hitting their lives and livelihoods. The impacts are becoming more deadly and more costly. In the past six years, extreme weather events have rocked the nation: the Black Summer bushfires of 2019–20; the disastrous North Queensland floods of 2019; the Lismore floods of 2022; and in 2025 the New South Wales mid-north-coast floods; mass bleaching events on the Great Barrier Reef and Ningaloo Reef; the devastating algal bloom that stretches over 4000 square kilometres off South Australia, laying waste to marine life along the coast – the list goes on. Catastrophes like these are exacerbated by climate change, caused in some part by emissions from Australia's huge coal and gas exports.

Despite the Paris Agreement, global greenhouse gas emissions are still rising. In June this year, sixty climate scientists published a report, *Indicators of Global Change 2024*, issuing another bleak warning that holding global warming to 1.5°C is likely out of reach. Lead author Professor Piers Forster from the University of Leeds made the simple point: "Climate policies and pace of climate action are not keeping up with what's needed to address the ever-growing impacts." The scientists warned that the next three years will be crucial in stopping this seemingly inexorable rise of emissions. That is the lifespan of the current federal parliament. In the last election, most Australians voted for candidates or parties promising action on climate change. Labor now has a thumping majority in the House of Representatives, the Greens hold the balance of power in the Senate, and independent candidates elected on strong climate platforms were mostly returned in their seats around the country. The parliament will debate Australia's emissions reduction targets for 2035 under the *Climate Change Act*. That debate needs to include why the most significant part of Australia's global carbon footprint, our fossil-fuel exports, is largely ignored in our national climate and environment laws.

SOURCES

3 third-largest single industrial greenhouse gas emitter: Jo Lauder, "Australia just approved Woodside's gas project until 2070. How could it happen?", ABC News online, 31 May 2025.

3 "the worst climate-polluting infrastructure": David Ritter, "Woodside ecocide: Gassing the future", *Australian Quarterly*, vol. 94, no. 1, January–March 2023.

3 "the Southern Hemisphere's largest gas carbon bomb": Kelly O'Shanassy, ACF Facebook campaign, 24 April 2024, facebook.com/story.php/?story_fbid=819134720247183&id=100064519881065&_rdr, accessed 30 July 2025.

3 6 billion tonnes: Bill Hare et al., "The full implications of the North West Shelf decision", Climate Analytics, 5 June 2025, p. 6, climateanalytics.org/publications/the-full-implications-of-australias-north-west-shelf-decision, accessed 30 July 2025.

4 "Climate risk matters": Alex Hillman in Brad Thompson, "Macfarlane withstands Woodside investor backlash over climate", *The Australian Financial Review*, 28 April 2023.

5 "Our climate strategy", "confidence", etc.: AGM address by Chair Richard Goyder and CEO Meg O'Neill, Woodside, 8 May 2025, woodside.com/docs/default-source/asx-announcements/2025/032-agm-address-by-chair-richard-goyder-and-ceo-meg-o'neill.pdf, accessed 30 July 2025.

7 "what's being done today": Darren Woods, "ExxonMobil CEO Darren Woods on what it takes to get to net zero", *Fortune*, 28 February 2024, fortune.com/2024/02/28/leadership-next-exxonmobil-ceo-darren-woods

9 "hard-edge trained": Andrew Forrest, Perth radio remarks reported in Hamish Hastie, "'Let's talk about Meg': Woodside wants Twiggy's Meg O'Neill remarks condemned", *WA Today*, 8 December 2023.

10 "The world is going to have to continue": Rex Tillerson, quoted in Tim Wyatt, "Exxon avoids climate change shareholder revolt led by Church Commissioners", *Church Times*, 3 June 2016.

11 "All of our investment decisions": Meg O'Neill, Woodside merger teleconference, 17 August 2021, woodside.com/docs/default-source/asx-announcements/2021-asx/woodside-merger-teleconference-transcript.pdf, accessed 30 July 2025.

12 "Before the ink is dry": Dan Gocher, "Woodside ignores COP26, accelerates emissions growth", ACCR media release, 15 November 2021.

12 "a bit of a jig": Scott Morrison, quoted in Jacob Greber, "Woodside gas project go-ahead prompts 'a bit of a jig' from Morrison", *The Australian Financial Review*, 24 November 2021.

12 "boon": Mark McGowan, quoted in "Thousands of jobs to be created as LNG development progresses", WA Government media statement, 22 November 2021.

19 "not a single LNG project": Department of Treasury, Budget Strategy and Outlook, Budget Paper No. 1, 2023–24, archive.budget.gov.au/2023-24/bp1/download/bp1_2023-24.pdf, accessed 30 July 2025.

19 "daylight robbery": David Pocock, quoted in Clint Jasper, "Australia missing out on $13 billion in royalty revenue from gas projects, report says", ABC News online, abc.net.au/news/2024-05-30/gas-royalties-missing/103907264.

20 "Man-made carbon emissions", "may amplify": Shell, *The Greenhouse Effect*, confidential report, released by the Climate Files, climatefiles.com/shell/1988-shell-report-greenhouse accessed 1 August 2025.

21 "the major role", etc: "Widespread carbon pricing is vital to tackling climate change", *Financial Times*, 1 June 2015 ft.com/content/682898fe-07e4-11e5-9579-00144feabdc0#axzz3bmvMIfbV.

21 "Our industry has": Peter Coleman, quoted in Peter Klinger, "Coleman not a coal man", *The West Australian*, 4 June 2015.

23 "if not for WA's natural gas", "Put simply", etc.: Roger Cook, address to the WA Energy Transition Summit, 17 November 2023.

25 "I'm not going to shackle": Roger Cook, quoted in Keane Bourke and Andrea Mayes, "WA Premier Roger Cook pulls back on WA climate change targets, says emissions may rise", ABC News online, 7 May 2025.

26 "globally, new fossil-fuel projects": Climate Change Authority, *Sector Pathways Review* 2024, 2024, p. 189.

29 "Premier must fix": Peter Coleman, "Premier must fix the EPA's carbon emissions mess", *The West Australian*, 9 March 2019.

29 "unworkable": Scott Morrison, in Lisa Cox, "WA's plan to curb emissions 'unworkable', says Morrison", *Guardian Australia*, 8 March 2019.

30 "The government did not support": Mark McGowan, WA Legislative Assembly, 13 March 2019.

31 "It's an annual dual-purpose social event": Mark Di Stefano, "Anthony Albanese, Peter Dutton gather in the court of Kerry Stokes", *The Australian Financial Review*, 20 October 2024.

31 "I also want to thank Kerry": Mark Di Stefano and Max Mason, "Inside Kerry Stokes' world of influence", *The Australian Financial Review*, 17 April 2023.

32 less than 8 per cent: P.C. Tinley, *Domestic Gas Supply in a Changing World: Inquiry into the WA Domestic Gas Policy: Final report*, WA Economics and Industry Standing Committee, August 2024, p. 52.

35 "This is beyond the pale": Madeleine King, interview with ABC Radio Perth, 2 August 2023.

35 "Wittingly or unwittingly": Roger Cook, quoted in Daile Cross, "WA premier lashes ABC in letter to Buttrose over Four Corners presence at protest", *WA Today*, 4 August 2023.

37 "a corporate villain": Mehreen Faruqi, "Bully-boy Woodside using its massive resources to intimidate and bankrupt peaceful protestors", The Greens, media release, 27 July 2023.

43 "carbon bomb": Piers Verstegen, *Woodside's Burrup Hub Carbon Bomb in Perspective*, Climate Safe Solutions with the Australian Conservation Foundation, March 2024.

48 "on the basis": Woodside Energy, "Strengthening connections", 6 January 2020, woodside.com/media-centre/news-stories/story/strengthening-connections, accessed 1 August 2025.

50 "It was considered": Daniel Thomas, Parliamentary Inquiry into the Juukan Gorge Caves Destruction, Joint Standing Committee on Northern Australia, 21 September 2020.

51 "A lasting impression": Ken Mulvaney, "Without them – what then? People, petroglyphs and Murujuga", in *Histories of Australian Rock Art Research*, ANU Press, 2022, p. 161.

52 "stand with": Karen Michelmore, "Protestors block Pilbara road over massive Woodside gas project", NITV, SBS Online, 24 November 2021.

53 "as I stand here": Peter Jeffries, *Destruction of 46,000-year-old Caves at Juukan Gorge*, Joint Standing Committee on Northern Australia, 2 November 2020.

54 "a constant threat": Benjamin W. Smith et al., "The impact of industrial pollution on the rock art of Murujuga, Western Australia", *Rock Art Research*, vol. 31, no. 9, 2022, p. 10.

55 "ensure that no air emissions": WA Environmental Protection Authority, Executive summary, *Perdaman Urea Project*, Report 1705, September 2021, p. iii.

56–7 "It's very pleasing": Roger Cook, in "Scientist expresses concern WA government department interfered with rock art report linked to North West Shelf approval process", ABC News online, 28 May 2025.

57 "disgrace": Friends of Australian Rock Art, Instagram reel, 27 May 2025, instagram.com/reel/DKJrMgDKp0P accessed 1 August 2025.

61 "Some of the conditions": Murray Watt, "North West Shelf: Report reveals Tanya Plibersek's unusual intervention after sharing of rock art info delayed", *The West Australian*, 18 June 2025.

63 "Now is not the moment": Jennifer Rayner, "A future gas strategy that sends us back to the future", Climate Council media release, 9 May 2024.

63 "The gas lobby's": John Grimes, in "2020 gas policy is a recipe to cook the planet", Smart Energy Council, 9 March 2024, smartenergy.org.au/2050-gas-plan-is-a-recipe-to-cook-the-planet accessed 1 August 2025.

64 "This Soviet-style policy": Kevin Gallagher, in Angela Macdonald-Smith, "Santos seeks project guarantees under 'Soviet-style' gas policy", *The Australian Financial Review*, 15 December 2022.

64 "the certainty they need": Jim Chalmers, Chris Bowen, Madeleine King and Ed Husic, Joint media release: "New Gas Code secures supply at reasonable prices for Australian users", 14 June 2023.

65 on course for warming of up to 2.6°C by 2100: The 2024 IEA report estimated the STEPS scenario having the world on course for warming of up to 2.4°C by 2100, but this may change again with the recent US policy reversals. See IEA, *World Energy Outlook* 2024, p. 20.

66 "Decisions by governments": IEA, *World Energy Outlook*, p. 20

66 from $72 billion to just $45 billion: Office of the Chief Economist, *Resources and Energy Quarterly*, Department of Industry, Science and Resources, March 2025, p. 56.

66 An investigation by Bloomberg reporters: Stephen Stapczynski, Spe Chen and Jin Wu, "How Japan ignored climate critics and built a global natural gas empire", *Bloomberg*, 30 August 2024.

67 "quiet quitting", etc.: Takayuki Ueda, quoted in Jacob Greber, "Australia's gas policies threaten world peace, says Japanese giant", *The Australian Financial Review*, 30 March 2023.

72 "strikes the right balance": Roger Cook, quoted in "Major milestone as environmental approvals reform accelerates", WA Government media statement, 14 August 2024.

74 "We are of the view": Roger Cook, quoted in Jesinta Burton, "'PM doesn't call me for permission': Cook downplays role in thwarted nature laws", *WA Today*, 3 December 2024.

75 levels not seen for 800,000 years: World Meteorological Organization, *State of the Global Climate Report* 2024, no. 1368, 2025, p. 1.

76 "a diverse and resilient portfolio": Meg O'Neill, Woodside Energy media release, 14 May 2025.

76 "Certainly, that includes": Amin Nasser, Speech to CERAWeek, Houston, 10 March 2025.

78 "is set to depress": International Energy Agency, *World Energy Outlook* 2024, October 2024, p. 50.

80 "a historic mistake": Bill Hare et al., "The full implications of the North West Shelf decision", Climate Analytics, June 2024, p. 4.

82 "Failure": International Court of Justice, *Obligations of States in Respect of Climate Change, Summary of the Advisory Opinion*, 23 July 2025, https://www.icj-cij.org/sites/default/files/case-related/187/187-20250723-sum-01-00-en.pdf, accessed 4 August 2025.

82 emissions cuts in the range of 65 to 75 per cent: Climate Change Authority, "Targets, Pathways and Progress issues paper released for consultation", media release, 11 April 2024.

83 "This is the biggest impact": Amanda McKenzie, "Labor's new environment laws won't be 'credible' unless new projects consider climate change, advocates warn", *Guardian Australia*, 19 June 2025.

83 1.5°C is likely out of reach: Piers M. Forster et al., "Indicators of Global Climate Change 2024: Annual update of key indicators of the state of the climate system and human influence", *Earth System Data Science*, vol. 17, no. 6, 2025.

83 "Climate policies": Piers Forster, "Scientists find three years left of remaining carbon budget for 1.5°C", University of Leeds website, 19 June 2025, leeds.ac.uk/news-global/news/article/5801/scientists-find-three-years-left-of-remaining-carbon-budget-for-1-5-c, accessed 1 August 2025.

HARD NEW WORLD

Correspondence

Lachlan Harris

The most confronting thing about reading Hugh White's *Hard New World* is the realisation that it's the things Donald Trump is getting right, not the multitude of things he's getting wrong, that are making a mess of Australia's defence and foreign policy settings. The fact that these settings are broadly bipartisan makes this realisation all the scarier.

White is no fan of Trump, and rightly condemns him as "narcissistic, cruel and avaricious." However, it's White's assessment that Trump's worldview "swims with the tide of history, not against it" that makes his essay an essential call to arms for Australia's political class. White reinforces this warning by reminding us that Trump's worldview is not an abrogation of his campaign commitments, it's a mirror image of "American voters' decisive rejection of the old idea of US global leadership."

White's message is clear: changes in the "Eurasian supercontinent" mean the US no longer has the incentive or the means to maintain strategic primacy in Asia. US voters and the US president have both worked this out, and there is little chance that a change of US political leadership will reverse this strategic reality. Trump's wrong about a lot but he's right about this, and the implications for Australia are profound.

Acknowledging this reality is difficult because a widespread belief in an Anglophone great power guaranteeing our security has been the bedrock of Australian strategic thinking since the day Captain Cook arrived. The consequence is a national strategic mindset that is the myopic inverse of Paul Keating's grand ambition: security *from* Asia, not in it. For many Australians, it has always and will always be thus. As White writes in his most provocative and most accurate sentence, "Donald Trump is doing us a favour by puncturing this complacent optimism." It's hard to read, but impossible to ignore.

White asserts that the primary consequence of this "favour" should be the long-overdue realisation that Australians "should free ourselves from the debilitating assumption that we cannot look after ourselves." Trump's uncouth honesty has, perhaps unwittingly, shattered this myth. As White argues, this means "our armed forces must be designed primarily to defend Australia." The critical implications for AUKUS are self-evident.

As an experienced strategic thinker, White has grounded his analysis on the foundation stone of necessity. For White, self-reliance is not an aspiration, but rather a mournful acknowledgement that "[i]t is not Australia but America that is walking away from the commitments it made in the ANZUS Treaty." Given the profound impact on our defence and foreign policy settings, White has rightly restricted his assessments to these fields.

However, thinking through the local political consequences of White's global strategic analysis, it's possible to perceive a barrage of secondary consequences for Australia springing from these global shifts. These consequences extend well beyond defence and foreign policy, encompassing the full range of policy challenges – economic, climatic and social – that Australia will face in a "post-American future." If White's primary consequences are grounded in the hard bedrock of strategic necessity, these secondary consequences must be planted in the soft ground of political opportunity.

White concedes that choosing to defend ourselves will be deeply confronting for our national leaders. He makes the case that necessity outranks risk. I would add to White's analysis by arguing that on the other side of this strategic pivot lies a rich seam of political opportunity for any Australian leader willing to mine it. Why? Because a pivot to self-reliance requires not just a profound reorientation of our defence and foreign policies but an ambitious reinvigoration of our economic, environmental and social policy reform agenda as well.

The prime minister of Canada, Mark Carney, and the German chancellor, Friedrich Merz, both recently won important election victories by breaking with their respective policy orthodoxy and placing national independence at the centre of their pitch. More importantly, both leaders were elected with strong mandates to undertake the ambitious domestic reforms required to achieve their strategic goals. Carney's "no turning back" warning and Merz's admission that he "never thought I would have to say something like this" suggest this political strategy only works when you go all in.

Winning for no reason is the scourge of modern politics. It creates listless governments that know what they oppose but have no idea about what they want to get done. By winning with purpose, Carney and Merz didn't just win elections;

they also won the chance to govern well. Australia has seen some great election campaigns in recent decades, but purposeful election victories have been few and far between.

A pivot to self-reliance is Australia's chance to change all that and gain the terminal velocity required to escape Donald Horne's "Lucky Country" curse. Once we are serious about standing on our own two feet, Australia will have to do more than just adjust our defence and foreign policy settings. We will also have to grow our economy, stabilise our climate and ensure we have the social cohesion needed to survive in the AI age. None of this will be easy, and at the heart of each of these challenges will be controversial policy reforms. Reducing the mismatch between the tax on labour and capital, accepting both economic and climatic trade-offs in our energy policy, being clear-eyed about well-planned population growth, and prioritising the housing needs of the young over the housing wants of the old are just some examples of the hard-edged reforms that may be required. None are popular; all may be necessary.

Australian politics is becalmed by an "if it ain't broke, don't fix it" mindset, and a "growth for growth's sake" argument that just hasn't cut through. Even more confoundingly, although economic growth, climatic stability and social cohesion are worthy ends in themselves, each has been in irreconcilable tension with the others. The result has been a political Gordian knot.

Self-reliance helps us cut that knot by giving ambitious policy reform advocates the one thing that has been missing in recent years: a reason why. The necessity of self-reliance is the why. A reason to undertake urgent economic, climatic and social policy reform, but also a reason why each of these ends must be balanced against the others. Without a north star, such compromises seem reductive; with one, they're strategic.

When strategic necessity and political opportunity align, elected leaders often rise to the occasion. Such is the temperamental genius of democracy. Australia's "post-American future" is one of these historic times. The only question now is which of our leaders will rise to meet the moment. The risks are immense, the path complex, but the reward is rare: the chance to join the ranks of Australia's truly great prime ministers.

Lachlan Harris

Correspondence

Emma Shortis

"Have you even said thank you to the president?"

For the United States' traditional allies, watching Vice President J.D. Vance and President Donald Trump treat Ukraine's President Volodymyr Zelenskyy with such aggressive contempt was a harrowing experience. The demand for gratitude as they threw Zelenskyy's people to the wolves while attempting to steal Ukrainian sovereign wealth and resources was a betrayal so deep it almost defies understanding.

President Joe Biden said that the United States, and the rest of the world along with it, sat at a historic inflection point. He was right. The America we thought we knew is gone.

Hugh White is one of the few people in this country who saw that coming, and saw it from a long way out. That his warnings have fallen on deaf ears is an indictment of the Australian foreign and security policy community. His latest essay is essential reading for that community, and for the Albanese government – which, as Hugh rightly points out, appears to have neither "the imagination to see what was happening [nor] the energy to respond."

And yet, since the essay was written, things have deteriorated. They will continue to do so.

With its aggressive imperial revival and its trashing of what is left of the international rule of law, the Trump administration is a direct threat to Australian and global security. We can no longer pretend, as the deputy prime minister continues to insist, that Australia has "shared values" with Trump's version of America. And yet "our leaders," as Hugh notes with evident and justified dismay, "are still in denial about all this."

Just as Hugh has long predicted, for the United States' traditional allies, a new reality is dawning. Australia has long been one of the United States' staunchest friends. Our governments have followed the US into nearly every war it has fought since the end of World War II. Australia went "all the way with LBJ" and followed the Bush administration into its disastrous wars in Afghanistan and Iraq, leaving only when America did. Some of that was driven by gratitude for American support during World War II – and some of it was driven by the sense that, in return, the United States would protect us again if the need arose.

More recently, that "protection" has come in the form of the AUKUS submarine pact – the biggest change in Australian defence policy for decades and the largest ever transfer of Australian sovereign wealth to another country. In January, the Australian government put down an $800-million deposit on what is projected to be a $368-billion deal. That deal is supposed to result in Australia getting nuclear-powered submarines with the assistance of the United Kingdom and United States. It will tie Australian sovereignty and defence decision-making to the United States for the rest of the century.

The British government has indicated that, in light of the Trump administration's trashing of NATO, it may turn away from the joint submarine deal to refocus on Europe. And in June, the Trump administration announced a review of the deal to ensure it fits the president's "America First" agenda. That review is incomplete, but it looks increasingly likely it will come back with demands for more money and a pre-commitment to conflict.

The Trump administration has made it quite clear that it does not care about America's allies. It has betrayed trust and confidence in a way many never thought possible. That the Australian government continues to insist that AUKUS is the only way forward is nothing less than, as Hugh puts it, "the perfect symbol of the failure of our entire political system to respond to a changed world."

Perhaps the Australian government should be grateful. Australia has, so far, successfully avoided the wrath of the Trump administration. While it has threatened Australia with tariffs and retaliatory action over our regulatory practices, it has not (yet) threatened to take our rare earth minerals or illegally annex our territory, as it has done to Ukraine, Gaza, Canada and Greenland. Australian diplomats and ministers are working around the clock to insulate this country from the worst excesses of the Trump administration, as they should. The stakes for Australia, and the United States' other allies, are incredibly high.

But the Australian people are not grateful. We are increasingly afraid. In March 2025, the Australia Institute surveyed 2000 Australians. Asked who they thought was a greater threat to global security, respondents were given three options. Twenty-seven per cent chose Vladimir Putin. The same number chose Xi Jinping. Thirty-one per cent chose Donald Trump. One in three Australians now view the leader of our most important security ally and the world's most important democracy as a bigger threat to world peace than the leaders of the world's two most powerful authoritarian states.

We now find ourselves in the desperately precarious situation, as Hugh sees it, of relying on a "balance of resolve" holding between these leaders – strongmen who must convince each other what they will and won't fight over. The United States under Trump, he argues, "lacks the clear resolve" to use nuclear weapons. While it is true that the president lacks resolve about most things (except, perhaps, a desire to protect himself and amass more wealth), it is also true that he changes his mind all the time, usually depending on whom he has spoken to last. He is deeply emotional, driven by ego and vengeance, and is easy both to charm and to provoke. This is missed by a realist understanding of international relations, which projects a certain kind of rationality and a consideration of consequence that does not always exist.

That projection of rationality, of cold calculation, allows much analysis to step around the moral questions at the core of these arguments. What would it mean to have the "resolve" to use nuclear weapons? And what would it mean for an Australian government to explicitly or implicitly support that resolve, as it did the Trump administration's illegal and unilateral bombing of Iran?

Once again, the Australian community is largely ahead of the government in its sense of the pressing nature of these questions. For very good reason, half of Australians feel less secure since Trump was elected in November 2024. By April 2025, 58 per cent of Australians thought Trump's election was a bad thing for Australia. Sixty-six per cent thought it was a bad thing for the world.

Polling during the Australian election campaign in May 2025 found that fifty-four per cent of Australians believed that Australia's interests are better served by a more independent foreign policy. By July 2025, 66 per cent said they would support a parliamentary inquiry into AUKUS.

In that sense, this essay could not come at a more critical time. Trump offers Australia an opportunity to fundamentally rethink our security – to let go of the myths and assumptions Hugh so clearly identifies.

There is a potentially seismic shift underway in Australian thinking about America. And it is not limited to us. In Germany – another of the United States' staunchest allies – the new chancellor, Friedrich Merz, has canvassed a new "independence from the USA." That was before Trump and Vance met Zelenskyy. In Denmark, too, opinion has shifted dramatically. Nearly half of Danes now see the United States as a threat – more than North Korea or Iran.

In April 2025, Pew surveyed people across twenty-four countries on their views of America and Trump. In nineteen of those countries, more than half of respondents lacked confidence in American leadership. In America's closest allies, the numbers were worse. In Canada, 77 per cent of people had "no confidence in Donald Trump to do the right thing in world affairs." In Germany, it was 81 per cent.

In South Korea, 67 per cent. In the UK, 62 per cent. This catastrophic loss of trust will be very difficult to repair.

Reagan's meeting with Gorbachev in Reykjavik in 1986 signalled the beginning of America's unipolar moment. Trump's ritual humiliation of Zelenskyy surely marked its end. The United States' traditional allies look on with sadness and trepidation. Holding on to that is essential. Perhaps the greatest and most lasting insight in Hugh's excellent essay is that "if we are to understand the world we live in," we must not lose "our sense of bewilderment and dismay."

The collapse of democracy and the rule of law in the United States is in no one's interests, least of all its own, and nor is the projection of that turmoil out into the world.

The humiliation of America's allies is America's humiliation too. It is a desperate end to a hope-filled beginning. But hope is not lost. It can be found in honesty, imagination and – as Hugh reminds us – ourselves. We now live in a post-American future. We can choose to make that future our own.

Emma Shortis

HARD NEW WORLD

Correspondence

Ali Wyne

In his classic defence of free speech, *On Liberty*, John Stuart Mill observed that one of the chief obstacles to the pursuit of objective truth is "a dead dogma" – a proposition that is widely accepted, yet poorly understood and rarely interrogated; absent vigorous, continued scrutiny, he explained, "the finer essence" of such propositions is lost, with only "the shell and husk" remaining.

Hugh White, the eminent Australian strategic thinker, offers a bracing critique of one such dogma in his essay. One that, he observes, "still dominates the thinking of Washington's old – pre-Trumpian – foreign policy establishment": that the United States must exercise "global leadership" to uphold what many US policymakers and scholars call "the rules-based international order." While his primary audience is in Canberra, which he believes must fundamentally reconceive its relationships with Beijing and Washington, his essay deserves careful consideration in the latter capital as well.

White contends that "the foundational cost–benefit calculus that underpins America's broad strategic posture has switched" for two reasons. First, its relative pre-eminence has diminished since the end of the Cold War. Second, so too has the salience of the core rationale that has motivated its postwar foreign policy: to forestall the emergence of a hegemon across Eurasia. While China is a multidimensional challenger, he concludes that it "will not be able to dominate Asia as a whole," let alone the far greater expanse of Eurasia; were it to try, he ventures, India, Russia and Europe would mobilise in resistance, with the United States joining a counterbalancing effort as needed. (White concludes that "we will see a global multipolar order in which a number of 'great powers' play more or less equal roles in shaping world affairs," but his own analysis makes one question which countries would make his list beyond the United States and China. He contends that "China will be the strongest power in East Asia and the Western Pacific by a very long way," ruling out India; observes that "on most measures, Russia hardly ranks as a great power"; and, as for Europe, ventures only that it has the "potential to coalesce as a fourth Eurasian great power.")

Strategic competition between the United States and China is and will likely continue to be most acute in Asia. White's outlook for the continent is unclear. He at one point envisions, plausibly, "a multipolar Asia, divided between two great powers and with a number of influential middle powers." Shortly thereafter, however, he stipulates that "with or without a war, America will soon withdraw from Asia." US attention to Asia has been fitful, and its economic agenda there lacklustre, but this judgement seems premature when one considers the deepening of America's military and technological relationships with countries including Australia, India, Japan, the Philippines and Vietnam.

White persuasively argues, though, that the United States must define a new role for itself in an increasingly complex and contested order. President Donald Trump's foreign policy offers one possibility. In an address in May 2025 at the Saudi–US Investment Forum, Trump intoned that "the so-called 'nation-builders' wrecked far more nations than they built – and the interventionists were intervening in complex societies that they did not even understand themselves." But if he has spotlighted one illusion – that the United States can remake the rest of the world in its image – he appears to have embraced another: that by dint of blunt coercion and bilateral dealmaking, he can impose his preferences on allies and adversaries alike without undercutting US influence over the long run.

Indeed, while key figures in his administration, including Vice President J.D. Vance and Secretary of State Marco Rubio, argue that Trump's "America First" worldview is an overdue adaptation to what they regard as emerging multipolarity, Trump's statements and actions do not reflect a commensurate modesty. Six months into his second term, he has insisted that Canada should be subsumed into the United States as its fifty-first state, pledged to annex Greenland and the Panama Canal as part of a new "manifest destiny," and upended the international economic order with his "Liberation Day" tariff campaign. Alternatively, given his predilection to change course, often contradicting himself in the process, one could posit that inconsistency is more operative than doctrine in shaping his foreign policy.

Even though China has yet to be a major focus of Trump's foreign policy, his actions have enabled it to present itself as an upholder of the current order – and the United States as a, if not the, principal revisionist. US allies and partners share – in principle, if not always to the same degree – many of Washington's apprehensions over Beijing's conduct. In Europe, those concerns centre on the deepening of Sino–Russian ties, the inability of European companies to compete with their Chinese counterparts in high-end manufacturing, and the ability of

China to translate economic influence across the continent into coercive power. In Asia, they revolve on China's intensifying pressure on Taiwan, its expansive claims across the South China Sea, and widespread assessments that it aspires to regional hegemony. Today, however, US allies and partners must be at least as worried about the incumbent power's trajectory. In view of Trump's re-election, they would be prudent to assume that some variant of naked transactionalism will periodically shape US foreign policy. As such, whether it issues polite requests or blunt demands, the United States will likely be less able to mobilise its diplomatic network against China over time.

Trump's mercurial temperament makes it hazardous to predict the direction of America's China policy over the coming years. White is probably correct that "no one anywhere near public office [in the United States] is willing to argue for a policy of accommodation" – at least not out loud – but it is important to spotlight members of Congress who are creating breathing room to reconsider America's China policy. In February 2025, for example, at the launch event for the Institute for America, China, and the Future of Global Affairs at Johns Hopkins University, Senator Andy Kim asserted that there is "still a lot of room for debate" on that policy. Elsewhere Congresswoman Sara Jacobs observed that "this isn't actually about maintaining American hegemony. This is about how we create the multipolar world that we are okay with. I think if we can focus on that latter idea, then it creates much more space for us to be able to work with the Chinese in the areas that we can, and stand up to them in the areas that we have to, without it necessarily becoming this all-encompassing conflict." Congressman Adam Smith concluded that "China is going to exist. We're going to exist … so we better figure out some way to peacefully coexist. So we need to build a frame for this world, not a frame for the 1950s, not a frame for the 1990s."

Ironically, the individual who has arguably done the most to create more political space for new thinking on America's approach to China is Trump himself (White observes that "on strategic questions, Trump really isn't a China hawk," even as he "has always been obsessed with China as an economic rival") – ironically, because it was his first administration that argued America's erstwhile policy had failed; that China is an adversary, not merely a competitor; and that President Xi Jinping is a Marxist-Leninist dictator who aims for his country to supplant the United States in Asia and in time the world. Critically, though, Trump did not endorse the high-profile documents and speeches that articulated those views. He criticised the size of China's trade surplus and empowered senior officials to enact a forceful agenda against China when he concluded that the COVID-19 pandemic could jeopardise his re-election prospects, but, unlike many of those advisers, he did not see strategic competition as a zero-sum, highly ideological contest unfolding across the world.

That chasm endures in his current term. At the end of May 2025, for example, in a speech at the Shangri-La Dialogue, US Secretary of Defense Pete Hegseth posited a Manichean struggle between Washington and Beijing, warning that China would "become a hegemonic power in Asia" unless the United States and its Asian allies and partners could forge "a strong shield of deterrence." In separate posts less than a week later, though, Trump stated that "I like President Xi of China, always have, and always will" and thanked Xi for inviting him to visit China.

The phrase "the Trump administration" is something of a misnomer, then, for it discounts the dissonance that often exists between Trump and his advisers on key issues, perhaps nowhere more evidently than on China policy. One can only imagine how vociferously Republican lawmakers would have criticised Barack Obama or Joe Biden had either of them called Xi a "dear friend" and ventured that the United States and China could "together solve all of the problems of the world." Because Trump uttered those words, however, they have been reluctant to criticise him.

The good news, then, is that he is expanding the Overton window on China policy. The bad news is that his own China policy is inchoate at best and often self-defeating. At least as concerning as his actions abroad are those he is taking at home, whether cutting funding for scientific research, driving away international students, or, most recently, signing a piece of legislation – the "One Big Beautiful Bill" – that is projected to increase both America's national debt and wealth inequality dramatically.

Amid intense speculation over how Trump's China policy will evolve over the next three and a half years, perhaps the most consequential unknown is how he will handle cross-strait tensions, with many observers fearing that Beijing may be preparing to quarantine or even blockade Taiwan. The worst-case scenario would be a full-scale attack. While Trump has admittedly evinced little interest to date in Taiwan's security, it would be unwise for China to assume that he would not respond to such an assault – not because he necessarily or even likely shares the widespread judgement among US observers that Taiwan's absorption into the mainland would prove fatal to America's strategic position in Asia, but because he resents any intimation that he is "weak." In addition, Trump is reliably unpredictable. Thus, despite campaigning for re-election on the promise of "no new wars," he circumvented Congress to authorise the bombings of three Iranian nuclear sites, a bold demonstration of US military power that none of his predecessors appears to have seriously contemplated.

Even if one were to accept White's conclusion that "there is now no serious chance that America can defend Taiwan from China," it does not necessarily follow that China's leaders are "so tempted to attack Taiwan." Rather, as he himself notes, "Chinese leaders may well decide that their best course is to sit back and wait for events to take their natural course." The People's Liberation Army (PLA) has not fought a war since 1979, and the turbulence in its top echelons suggests that Xi, despite reportedly instructing the PLA to have the capacity to launch an attack on Taiwan by 2027, lacks confidence in its ability to execute an amphibious landing – one of the hardest military manoeuvres of all. Meanwhile, Russia's struggles in Ukraine underscore that would-be aggressors should not underestimate the ingenuity and resilience of their opponents.

Still, the challenge of ensuring that strategic competition between the United States and China does not culminate in armed confrontation will not go away. White is correct that Washington cannot credibly propose to "'manage' competition with Beijing while refusing to accommodate any of its ambitions." While the United States abstractly acknowledges that China deserves a growing role in the international order, it is difficult to think of a specific exercise of power on China's part in recent years that US policymakers have deemed acceptable. The converse is also true: Chinese officials reflexively deem virtually any assertion of US influence to be part of a campaign of containment. Both powers will have to eschew maximalist conceptions of their respective national interests if they are to achieve a stable equilibrium in Asia.

US observers need not agree with all of White's arguments to appreciate the importance of his essay: when a leading strategic thinker in one of America's closest allies exhorts his country to "work out how to make our way, for the first time in our history, in an Asia no longer made safe for us by a great and powerful friend" – going so far as to advocate a "post-alliance relationship" – Washington should take heed. As worried as its allies and partners are about what the next three and a half years of Trump's second term will bring, they fear, more broadly, that leaders in both parties are increasingly muddled in their understanding of and recommendations for adapting to today's geopolitical upheaval.

Ali Wyne

HARD NEW WORLD

Correspondence

James Curran

Since the publication in 2010 of *Power Shift*, his first Quarterly Essay, Hugh White can rightly claim vindication for his consistent argument that America's enthusiasm for maintaining hegemony in East Asia would be eroded. White has played a key part in a broader debate over the hard questions pressing upon the nation's and the region's strategic future – indeed, his role has arguably been much more important than that of any of the Australian defence or foreign policy think tanks. Need further proof be given of his success in disturbing the conventional wisdom than the shrill responses it has often provoked? No analyst can be right all the time or on everything, but from a standing start White foresaw China's growing strengths and the implications for America's posture in Asia, along with the consequences for long-established habits of mind and practice in Australia.

Two important questions now arise from White's latest essay, *Hard New World*. The first relates to how Australia thinks about the Asia-Pacific post-American military and economic hegemony, and especially the implications for our alliance with the United States. The second is even more challenging: what are the strategic terms on which Australia might engage China in the future? To call for greater defence self-reliance through the purchase of more drones and long-range missiles is one thing, but the larger basis on which Canberra deals with Beijing involves trade relationships, and whether Australia, along with Japan, South Korea and others, continues to shore up and expand the multilateral trading architecture on which regional interdependence so heavily relies. It also concerns how Australia handles a situation where its trade with China may decline. And with 2020 in mind, how would we cope with renewed Chinese economic coercion in the absence of the current close partnership with the United States? Multilateralism, it must be hoped, will be an antidote to the binary geopolitics of a "new Cold War." But it will be extremely difficult to achieve in an environment of mercantilism and trade war.

The post-American future is already here, so White's point, also delivered pungently by Paul Keating, was well made at least fifteen years ago. But short of Washington deciding that the costs of war with China are too great, as White has long argued, there is unlikely to be a dramatic moment of closure for the *Pax Americana* in Asia: no last helicopter taking off from the US Embassy, as in Saigon in 1975, or transport plane lifting off from the chaos, as in Kabul in 2021. It is more likely to be a longer winding-down.

And it is not yet clear that the Trump administration *will* accelerate American withdrawal from the region. We are yet to see the full deck of geopolitical cards dealt out by this White House, but allies are again being pressured to sign on to America's mission of containing China's rise: witness not only Secretary of Defense Pete Hegseth's call for Asian partners to increase their military spending, but also his pointed dismissal of those hedging between close economic ties with Beijing and tight security links with Washington. Yet how can those partners do otherwise when the Chinese market is so critical? Even if allies take no heed of his admonition, US–China strategic competition will create its own turbulent forcefield, with Indonesia, Japan, Korea and India each trying to find stability and security within the hurricane. That is likely to bring unforeseeable twists and turns over coming decades. So Australia has to think about new relationships beyond the dominant paradigm of Canberra home alone and clinging to a great-power protector.

Building a "post-alliance relationship" with Washington, as White implores us to do, will not be straightforward. There are no maps or clear coordinates with which to plot such a path. White has raised the prospect: he now needs to articulate how such a path can be pursued. In another era, Alfred Deakin once referred to the "stubbornly British nature of Australians." If this is translated to Australian attitudes to America today, the national security elite is even more deeply habituated to "alliance maintenance." Australia, as the response of political elites to the end of *Pax Britannica* in the late 1960s shows, does not do "end of empire" moments particularly well. There was at least a decade of handwringing about what many held to be the "unthinkable" end of Britishness before both sides of politics grasped the nettle of comprehensive engagement with Asia.

White urges Canberra to adopt the "Singapore model," in which greater self-reliance coexists with a close defence relationship with America. But Australia's ties to the United States are fundamentally different from those of Singapore, and Singapore could not be a significant military contributor to the defence of Taiwan or the Western Pacific. Across the economic, cultural, defence, foreign affairs and intelligence spheres, there is an intimacy between the US and Australia not easily untangled, a result of the past two decades in particular of deepening military integration. And if a clumsy, rapid and unilateral uncoupling was initiated by Australia, Trumpian reprisals could be harsh. White is understandably frustrated with the inability of successive governments to articulate a new version of the relationship, but how ought they wisely proceed? For Australian leaders merely to posture publicly could be even more dangerous and ultimately costly, a situation reminiscent of the Whitlam years and all too evident in the Morrison government's dealings with China. Even if Washington initiated the change, it would take some time to effect, probably years when we consider our dependence on American weapons, including their maintenance and next-generation development.

Preceding any Australian move, there would need to be an estimate of the short and long-term objectives of a reduction in military integration with the United States. It is not clear that this could be kept secret from Washington. If not, some kind of discussion would need to occur. That needs a safe pair of hands, but whether the national security elite in Canberra, so acculturated to the alliance as a permanent way of life, could conduct this kind of discussion is a genuine question. But at its core must be a brutally frank assessment of the strategic assistance Australia provides to the US and of what the US might, in a vastly different relationship, provide to Australia.

What needs to be measured too is how much the US military and intelligence presence in Australia is central to Trump's emerging relationship with China and whether it really is a bargaining chip of substance. And if Trump should concede to China's ultimate takeover of Taiwan amid a slow withdrawal of the US military from East Asia, what then? The same question concerning US bases is now being asked by Japan and the Philippines, which are even more crucial to US warfighting. And if Korea is the satellite that falls into China's orbit, what are the consequences of that? White assumes the US will cop a hiding if it intervenes to protect Taiwan. But if the US threatens force without actually having to use it, and Australia has ruled out its support and use of bases in the conflict, the scenario may be quite different. Hence Australia's major aim should be preventing a conflict over Taiwan.

Given the genuine unpredictability of the Trump team, might a more prudent course lie in articulating more clearly Australian sovereign rights or in demurring on US action on Taiwan that might assume Australian collaboration? Canberra could raise genuine issues about the UK delays in AUKUS submarine design, and the problems Australia faces in crewing Virginia-class submarines, if indeed they are transferred to Australia by the US under the current terms of the AUKUS agreement. Both the Morrison and Albanese governments have not made a sufficient public argument to the Australian people, or indeed to Washington, about the implications of AUKUS for Australian sovereignty or what it might entail in a future conflict. Sending these messages to the US will require considerable diplomatic finesse, if not guile. And it would need to be done while emphasising aspects of the partnership that Canberra wants to maintain: access to US weapons and weapons development, US intelligence and a range of other defence and diplomatic support.

White at several points stresses that Australia needs to "find our own way" with Beijing, but what would that entail? A solid case can be made that Australia has been finding its own way with China on trade since the height of the Cold War, a way that provoked disquiet in Washington. US military power did Australia no good when last China leaned on this country with its punitive trade restrictions during the Morrison government.

Trade with China is a critical element that could become more or less important. To sell more highly processed or manufactured goods to China, Australia would have to opt for deeper investment and economic integration. As it is, Australia and China's longstanding economic complementarity requires a large-scale refit. Over the coming few decades, the trade in iron ore and energy will need huge transformation in light of both nations' climate goals. The warnings are stark if Australia does not get this right. A report by the ANU's East Asian Bureau of Economic Research in 2024 argued that "that there are many technologies necessary for the clean energy transition in which China's research and development efforts are world leading and that failure to cooperate closely with China in these areas will see Australia fall away from the climate technology frontier and miss significant opportunities for economic prosperity in the clean energy industrial transformation." China's decarbonisation agenda, then, has major implications for Australia's continued wellbeing and prosperity. Informed projections are that "Australia's coal and liquefied natural gas exports could fall by 16 and 18 per cent respectively by 2050 due to China's transition to carbon neutrality." Indeed, those falls are "likely to be much larger under realistic scenarios." Absent strategies to work with China's carbon-neutral industrial future, Australia's influence and powerful complementarity will decline sharply.

In addition, Canberra must deal with China's desire for reform of its role in the global trading system. Beijing wants to be part of the Comprehensive and Progressive Agreement for Trans-Pacific Partnership, and now projects itself, somewhat hypocritically, as the defender of the multilateral trading rules and economic openness. Can Australia hope to shape these impulses into a positive force in global trade?

White says that China is ruthlessly "transactional," which is true, though all foreign policy relationships are essentially transactional and Trump gives new meaning to that. A case can be made that Australia's principal external relationships in the postwar period, except with Indonesia, have all been to a greater or lesser extent "transactional." It is what drove the repair of relations with Japan in the late 1950s and the economic complementarity of Australia and China since the iron ore trade took off in the 1980s. It has been central to the operation of the US alliance since the Iraq war: Australia has provided increasing access to intelligence facilities, airfields, logistics hubs and, soon enough, submarine bases; while the US has given us defence equipment and materiel. It is true that the alliance's history is punctuated by moments when Australia felt it did not get sufficient return on its investment – especially in tense moments with Indonesia over Confrontation in the 1960s and over East Timor in the late 1990s – but the transactional impulse has been an abiding feature of how Australia conducts international business and expresses its international personality.

All of this raises the inevitable question of what Australia's credible alternatives are. What is obvious is that Australia cannot let all its options hang off the US alliance in some vain hope that "regional strategic equilibrium" is achievable. US primacy is not coming back. Some kind of new connective tissue is needed for Australia in the region, building on cooperation with Japan, Korea, India and Southeast Asia. Not a quasi-NATO, of course – but the region is poorer for lack of a mechanism for crisis management. That will also require building multilateral cooperation with China on what Gareth Evans calls "global and regional public goods": everything from climate action to arms control, terrorism to pandemics. These are among the many and increasingly challenging pieces of statecraft needed to recast Australia's position in an incoherent and unsteady world.

James Curran

Correspondence

Susannah Patton

Hugh White's proposition that Australia is inevitably torn between its US alliance and the opportunity of true engagement with Asia has much in common with the claim that Australia has turned its back on Paul Keating's idea of "security in Asia." The problem with both arguments is that their proponents appear unwilling to look with fresh eyes at the state of Australia's current relationships in Asia. The assumption is always that we are doing badly compared to the good old days of the 1980s and 1990s. In fact, there's a strong case that Australia's relationships with the important countries of our region (China aside) are at an all-time high.

Consider the relationship with India – historically marked by Cold War divergence and mutual suspicion. Today, the relationship – since 2020, a comprehensive strategic partnership – is characterised by much closer strategic dialogue, including an annual leaders' meeting (one of just two such regular meetings for the Indian side) and a 2+2 meeting of foreign and defence ministers. While White dismisses the Quad as toothless, India, Japan, Australia and the United States participate in Exercise Malabar; behind the scenes, cooperation in tracking Chinese naval activity in the Indian Ocean has grown steadily. And consider this: in 2013 there were no direct flights between Australia and India. Today there are around thirty a week.

Earlier this year, India's forthright foreign minister, S. Jaishankar, put it this way: "A decade ago, if I had stood here and told you all that Australia would actually be amongst our closest political friends, our strongest security partners, a country with whom we would have a Free Trade Agreement, whose University would be among the first to actually set up an establishment in India – in fact, if I told you that we would have many more things to discuss other than cricket – I don't think any of you would have believed me."

Australia's strategic alignment with Japan is also at a high point. The two countries now have a reciprocal access agreement, allowing new cooperation, and in 2022 they signed an ambitious joint declaration on security. While there are numerous examples of new combined activities between the two countries' defence forces (including reciprocal deployments of F-35A joint strike fighters and Japan's regular participation in US force posture initiatives in Australia), discussion continues on the scope, objectives and forms of enhanced operational cooperation. Japan's defence minister, Nakatani Gen, has described Australia as a "quasi-ally," a reflection of Japan's view that Australia is its most important security partner after the United States.

In Southeast Asia, too, Australia is as well placed as it has ever been. The relationship with Indonesia was for many years described as a roller-coaster, with lows caused by disputes over agriculture, people-smuggling and spying. Today, the relationship is stable – the last major disruption to ties was in 2015, when Indonesia executed two Australian citizens. In the decade since, ups and downs have continued. It's no secret that Indonesia was unhappy when Australia announced the AUKUS partnership in 2021. And of course, White is right to point out that the defence cooperation agreement is far short of a security alliance. But at the practical level, defence cooperation has grown, with Australia deploying tanks and fighter aircraft to Indonesia to join multilateral and bilateral exercises. It's noteworthy also that an agreed outcome of Anthony Albanese's recent visit to Indonesia was the establishment of a new maritime dialogue and cooperation.

Elsewhere in Southeast Asia, Australia continues to have close, though quiet, defence cooperation with Malaysia, including using Malaysian Airforce Base Butterworth to fly P-8A surveillance flights over the South China Sea. The Singapore Armed Forces deploys approximately 6000 personnel each year to Australia to training ranges in Queensland and Western Australia, part of a quid pro quo granting Australia access to defence facilities in Singapore. In 2024 Vietnam – which sees Australia in the top tier of its partners – deployed a naval vessel to a multilateral exercise in Australia, the first time it has done so to any Western country.

White is right that diverging approaches to the United States and China place a ceiling on how closely Canberra can align with some Southeast Asian countries, such as Indonesia and Malaysia. Clearly, we will not be signing a security alliance with either country in the foreseeable future.

Yet the information I have provided on the state of Australia's current ties with the region, including on defence and security, suggests that the "ceiling" is much higher than White says. He claims that Australia's "primary aim has been to urge our neighbours to side with America against China" and that Australia "will not build the relationships we need in the decades ahead by conceiving our relationships entirely as a zero-sum contest between America and China for regional primacy." There is simply no evidence for this (is the same claim ever made of staunch US ally Japan?). Instead, Australia's approach, especially under the current foreign minister, Penny Wong, has been focused on investing in the relationships on their own terms and insulating them to the extent possible from the impact of US–China competition.

And finally, to White's claim that Australia is making life harder for Pacific Islands countries by forcing them to adopt our binary approach to China. Australia's engagement with the Pacific Islands countries is far from perfect and will always be characterised by power asymmetry. But would the region really be better off if Australia returned to its pre-2016 approach of benign neglect? And if, instead of giving alternatives to China's economic and security offerings, Canberra simply allowed the Pacific Islands region to become a Chinese lake? If the leaders of Fiji, Papua New Guinea or Tuvalu agreed that Australia was making their lives harder, they would not have agreed to security deals with Australia. Do the nearly one-third of all Tuvaluans who applied to migrate to Australia under the pathway offered through the Falepili Union agree that Australia is making their lives harder?

Lest my comment appear overly complacent or too congratulatory of the current government, let me say that I don't believe the above achievements have arisen simply because of clever diplomacy on Australia's part. If anything, Australian diplomacy outside the Pacific is rather less creative and ambitious today than in the past. Instead, the positive trends in these relationships are structural. While the level of strategic alignment varies greatly (from Japan at one end of the spectrum to the countries of mainland Southeast Asia at the other), all are given impetus by shared concerns: about China's growing regional influence, the reliability of the United States, and the need for a diversity of partnerships.

I'm also not claiming that these relationships amount to a concerted effort to balance against China that will have a material effect on the balance of power in Asia. But if White is right and we are heading for a multipolar Asia, then Australia is not nearly so isolated and preoccupied by its alliance with the United States as he claims. In fact, our relationships and the focus of successive governments on Australia's immediate regional neighbours will work in our favour, whatever is to come. Most importantly, there is no evidence that we must pre-emptively distance ourselves from America to advance our position in Asia.

Susannah Patton

Correspondence

Mark Edele

Hugh White is right. We are facing the end of the world as we knew it since 1991. We are in the middle of a shift today, and we do not know the outcome. This age of strategic chaos is potentially frightening, and many retreat into wishful thinking. Not only do we not know what will come next; all our reflexes and sentiments have been formed in a different era. White's analysis provides a vision of what lies ahead. He is to be congratulated for the clarity of his analysis.

In this emerging new world (dis-)order we need to urgently rethink our relationship with the United States, as White stresses. This will mean pulling out of AUKUS before we throw good money after bad. It is far from clear that the US has the will or the capacity to defend us. We should proceed on the assumption that it does not. Hence, we need to develop an Australian sovereign defence capability. White's *How to Defend Australia* gives one vision of how this might look; Sam Roggeveen's *Echidna Strategy* offers another. They agree on a central point: Australia needs to build a defence force which can deny an adversary the ability to approach it with hostile intent; at the very least, we need to increase the cost to the extent that an attack will not be worth it. It is time to set a clear strategic direction: the Australian Defence Force is not a support act to the US Armed Forces. Its primary function is to defend Australia. Currently, it is not equipped to do so on its own. *Hard New World* provides a useful sketch of how this could change.

I have more reservations about White's account of Russia's role in the world. I have long maintained that Russia is not a great power. It is a resource-extractive middle power at the edge of Europe and Asia, poised to decline further as the current regime has done nothing to prepare for decarbonisation. It has great-power delusions, because it has never come to terms, as a society and a culture, with the end of the imperial phase of its history. At the beginning of his essay, White seems to agree. China, India and "Europe" (presumably a shorthand for the EU plus the UK) are the three powers of consequence in the Europe–Asia region. Russia, by contrast, is a regional middle power keen to assert a great-power status it does not currently have. Most explicitly, White writes: "On most measures, Russia hardly ranks as a great power in comparison with America, China, Europe or even India." Its war against Ukraine is a gambit "to re-establish itself" as a great power. This gambit relies on conventional military power flanked by nuclear threats.

But Putin's willingness to brandish his nuclear arsenal in the face of opposition allows a slow slippage throughout the essay from acknowledging the reality of Russia's strategic weakness to treating it as a great power. By page 47, White describes Russia as "a fellow great power in a multipolar world," alongside China and the US. Ten pages later it appears as one of the great powers to balance China (its principal supporter today), alongside India and Europe. This is a possible but unlikely outcome of the transformation of the world system we witness today.

As Stephen Fortescue wrote in 2017, Russia cannot afford to be a great power but it can cause a lot of damage trying to be one. Damage is currently being inflicted, and the chief victim is Ukraine. But the outcome is still uncertain: whether Russia will emerge as a great power in the hard new world of the future will depend to a significant extent on how this war ends. So far, Russia has demonstrated that it can deter Europe and the US from direct participation, but that it is unable to subdue a much smaller, much less populous and much poorer neighbour. Russia has neither won the war nor successfully asserted its great-power status.

There are two ways in which Russia could become a great power again: it could win the war against Ukraine, or it could successfully negotiate a peace deal which gives it what it wants: a guaranteed sphere of influence in Eastern Europe. It seems that White believes the latter is somehow inevitable. It is not. It is true that by the summer of 2023 the war had transformed into one of attrition. This could have opened the door to negotiations; it did not. White blames Ukraine and its allies for this failure, a position reminiscent of President Trump's at the start of this year. Since then, of course, even the American president has realised what Russia specialists have long argued: Russia is not willing to negotiate. Putin thinks he is winning the war, even if slowly and painfully. He does not mind playing a long game and thinks he can wait "the West" (his term) out.

The two possible outcomes, then, are not a Russian victory and a negotiated peace, but Ukraine's complete surrender and a frozen long-term conflict. Only in the case of the former will Russia emerge as a great power. It is not at all clear how nuclear weapons will help it achieve that outcome.

As White points out, Russia is likely to use nuclear weapons if confronted with devastating defeat. A march on Moscow by a Ukrainian tank column would certainly trigger a nuclear strike. But equipping Ukraine to stop Russia from taking more of Ukraine is unlikely to lead to the same outcome. Russia does not face a devastating defeat every time Putin rattles his nuclear sabre. Putin is a keen student of Stalin, who memorably said that atomic bombs only frighten those with weak nerves. He uses nuclear threats because he thinks his opponents outside Ukraine are easily scared. In the over three years of war against Ukraine, Putin has threatened nuclear strikes repeatedly. He has never made good on this threat, partly because he has not faced the prospect of a devastating defeat, partly because he ponders the consequences of such a move.

Russia is not likely to face a devastating defeat in its war against Ukraine. The only force which tried to march on Moscow was that of Putin's own Yevgeny Prigozhin. Ukraine does not intend to destroy the Russian state. Until recently, it planned to chase the Russians out of Ukraine. Now, the Ukrainian government seems to have settled on the lesser but more achievable goal of halting the advance and saving the over 80 per cent of Ukraine it still controls. The task for Ukraine's friends now is to help with this task and rebuild a prosperous country in these de facto borders once they are secured.

There are other forces constraining Russia. Pressure from friendly outsiders is one. Russia's greatest friend, China, has made it very clear that it does not support a nuclear escalation. Simple geography is another constraint. Anybody who lived in St Petersburg in the 1990s (as Putin did) will remember Geiger counters at suburban train stations, where mushroom collectors could check their bounty for radiation. This was because of the long-term consequences of the 1986 Chornobyl nuclear disaster. A nuclear strike on Ukraine's territory would have long-term consequences for life in Russia as well, and Putin knows this. Finally, there are domestic political and ideological reasons to hold back: striking alleged military targets in Kyiv with conventionally armed drones is one thing; nuking what Russians call "the mother of all Russian cities" is quite another.

Like any good strategist, White is of course not just describing reality as we can observe it today. He is thinking several steps ahead. In his analysis, Ukraine has already lost the war; Russia has successfully re-established itself as a great power because the rest of the world has bowed to its nuclear threats and left Ukraine in the lurch. That is one possible future, but far from the only one. Today, it seems much more likely that the war will continue and eventually freeze into a continuing stalemate. In this future, Russia would remain what it is today: a regional power with unrealistic ambitions, a spoiler nation rather than a great power. Given Putin's maximalist demands, a third future – a negotiated peace – is theoretically possible but practically unlikely.

Ukraine is not the only place where White's analysis is ahead of the current state of affairs. The same is true for the global (dis-)order in general. His vision of the near future is one of great-power competition. It is the kind of world mainstream international relations theory is good at constructing, a system where several great powers jostle for domination and maybe find some kind of equilibrium: the United States, China and India in the Asia-Pacific; Russia, China and Europe in the Europe–Asia region. (We read nothing of Africa and little about the Middle East.) Smaller powers need to find their way in the system of power drawn up by this great-power dynamic.

This vision is one possible outcome of the current transformation of the global system. However, there is a different possible future: one in which smaller powers, like Australia, will play a major role. As a middle power and a democracy, Australia has an interest in building a global alliance of democracies as a break on the ambitions of great powers. Elsewhere, I have described this as a global coalition of the willing. This can and should begin in our region. We are surrounded not by great powers but by small democracies. White is right that we need to finally find security in the Asia-Pacific, not from it. But Asia is not one place. There are democratic nations like Japan, South Korea and, yes, Taiwan, and there are dictatorships like North Korea and China. Many Pacific nations have domestic problems with their democracies, but they are still much closer to our political sensibilities than autocracies like China or Russia. We need to build strong alliances with our democratic neighbours so we can confront, together, both the dictatorial and the imperial challenge of our hard new world.

Such a regional alliance of democracies could then also extend more broadly to nations with an interest in a world not dominated by a few nasty great powers: democracies in Europe, Africa and the Americas. Such an alliance could combine a commitment to international law, mutually beneficial trade agreements, defence coalitions and political solidarity. This is not an alternative to serious discussions about defence, as such an alliance of middling democracies will have to be armed to the teeth to keep predatory powers at bay.

Crucially, this world needs to be built without the United States. As White correctly points out, the US has too many problems at home. It can no longer lead the free world, and it does not want to. Indeed, we can be far from sure that by the end of the Trump era it will still be part of the free world at all. Australia will be, and it should take the lead in building a future where small and mid-sized democracies help balance the powers of the world's behemoths.

Like White's vision of the post-American globe, this would be a multipolar world. But democratic alliances would be one of the poles, and middle powers like

Australia would be strong players. We had better build it, because otherwise we will be in the position where we need to suffer what we must from great powers who will do as they will.

Mark Edele

Correspondence

Brendan Taylor

Hugh White has done more than anyone to make Australians think seriously about power in Asia. He saw, well before it became conventional wisdom, that the US-led order was passing, that China's rise would shake the region's foundations, and that Australia would face more difficult strategic choices than it had for generations. His latest Quarterly Essay, *Hard New World*, continues that essential work, urging Canberra to confront the reality of a multipolar Asia and the limits of old habits.

I agree with much of that assessment. But I want to take Hugh's argument a step further – and, in some respects, in a different direction. He sees Australia adjusting to a single, emerging regional order. I argue we must prepare for several. Asia is not shifting neatly from one system to another. It is instead evolving through a series of overlapping strategic phases: from bipolarity to tripolarity and then to something more complex still. Each phase will bring its own logic, its own risks and its own demands. The challenge for Australia is not just to adapt but to keep adapting – and to recognise when the regional balance has shifted.

Over the past half-century – the blink of an eye, strategically speaking – we have already passed through three distinct systems: Cold War bipolarity, post–Cold War unipolarity, and now US–China bipolarity. Each had its own strategic logic and demanded a different response from Australia. Yet successive governments have not always met those demands with clarity or coherence. Often, we have muddled through, relying on good fortune and inherited assumptions. That approach is unlikely to suffice in the decades ahead. If anything, the pace of change is accelerating, and with each power shift the strategic environment will impose new and different demands on Australian policy. The coming half-century will not bring a single new order but a succession of overlapping ones: a tense bipolar Asia in the 2020s and into the 2030s; a more fluid tripolarity in the 2030s and 2040s, as India's strategic weight and influence grows; and a looser multipolar structure by mid-century, as Indonesia enters the Asian balance as a great power. We must be prepared to operate across all three.

The great Australian international relations scholar Hedley Bull once warned that Canberra is often slow to grasp strategic change. In his famous 1974 essay "Australia and the Great Powers in Asia," he argued that the bipolar balance between the United States and the Soviet Union, which had shaped Australian thinking in the 1960s, was already giving way to a more complex quadrilateral Asian power structure, involving China and Japan as well. That strategic lag was evident in Australia's 1965 decision to commit combat troops to Vietnam – an act rooted in Cold War logic at a time when the regional balance was already beginning to shift. Bull's central insight was that Canberra's foreign and strategic policies remained attuned to an older order and that it was too slow to adjust to the new one forming around it.

That risk remains with us today. While great-power war – often the clearest catalyst for systemic transition – remains a very real possibility in Asia, strategic orders typically don't change overnight. They shift more gradually, as new powers rise and the balance adjusts. But that doesn't make the changes less real. Over time, the old order gives way to something quite different – not all at once, but often in stages. If we fail to see each stage for what it is, we risk making the wrong choices for the one we're actually in. With each new entrant or assertive state, the regional balance is not simply redistributed – it is reconfigured. If we treat the coming decades as one long transition to a new order, as Hugh does, we risk misreading the structure of the system we're in and building policy for the wrong one.

We are already living in a bipolar Asia. Power is concentrated in two poles – the United States and China – whose rivalry increasingly defines the region's military balance, trade patterns, trade and technology competition, and the flashpoints most likely to trigger conflict. Bipolar systems can be relatively stable, but they are also tense. And unlike the Cold War system, this structure lacks clear ideological fault lines, well-established rules of the road, or the crisis-management mechanisms that helped keep earlier confrontations from escalating.

Australia has already begun to feel the pressure. We continue to double down on our alliance with the United States through initiatives such as AUKUS and expanding American military access to Australian territory – prompting growing fears that we could be drawn into a conflict not of our choosing. That anxiety has only deepened since Donald Trump's return to the Oval Office. His transactional view of alliances, disregard for multilateralism, and ambiguous stance on extended nuclear deterrence have renewed doubts about US reliability not just in policy circles but also among publics across Asia.

Hugh is right to argue that we can no longer rely on America as we once did. But we must also acknowledge that the United States may not simply leave Asia, as Hugh anticipates. It remains a formidable actor – deeply divided at home, yes, but still the world's top military spender by a considerable margin, with unmatched power projection capabilities and a sprawling network of regional allies and partners. Should it choose to remain engaged, it has the capacity not only to shape Asia's security order for decades to come, but also to act as a spoiler. As the realist scholar John Mearsheimer has argued, great powers tend not only to dominate their own regions but also to prevent rivals from dominating theirs. A full American withdrawal would likely invite Chinese regional hegemony, and no US administration has yet accepted that prospect.

Bipolarity is likely to shape Asia for the remainder of the 2020s and into the 2030s. However long it ultimately lasts, this system demands that Australia not treat it as a waiting room for a future multipolar order, or rush toward defence self-reliance on the assumption that the United States will soon withdraw. We must read the structure of the system we are in, and act accordingly. That means recognising the constraints and risks of entrenched great-power rivalry – including the dangers of overdependence and premature decoupling alike – and ensuring that our defence and diplomacy remain calibrated to the realities of a still-active alliance in an increasingly contested region.

A tripolar Asia will bring a different set of challenges. As India's weight grows, Australia will need to recalibrate its assumptions about alignment and influence. Strategic choices that made sense in a bipolar system – such as bloc-building or binary balancing – may carry less weight in a more fluid, triangular configuration. India's interests won't always align with those of Washington or Canberra. The risks of misreading such a system are not new. In the early 1970s, it was China's sudden tilt towards the United States – not any Soviet manoeuvring – that fundamentally reshaped the Cold War order, transforming a rigid bipolar contest into something far less predictable. Australia responded with rare foresight. Gough Whitlam, then leader of the Opposition, led an ALP delegation to China in July 1971, just as Henry Kissinger was making his secret visit to Beijing. After winning office the following year, Whitlam swiftly moved to normalise diplomatic relations with the People's Republic. In a tripolar Asia, retaining that kind of strategic initiative – the capacity to read regional currents clearly and act at the right moment – may matter more than formal alignments.

Eventually, Asia may become truly multipolar – not dominated by any one power but shaped by a wider distribution of influence among China, the United States, India and Indonesia. Such systems are often even more unpredictable.

Alliances and alignments become looser. Smaller players are more likely to act opportunistically. Miscalculation becomes more probable.

Hugh rightly anticipates that India and, in time, Indonesia will become key poles in a future multipolar Asia. But what that multipolarity looks like – and what it will demand of Australia – is less fully developed in *Hard New World*. The entry of each new great power will not simply add another player. It will reshape the logic of the system itself. And with each shift, Australia's strategic dilemmas will grow more complex. The choices we face in a bipolar system are not the same as those in a tripolar or multipolar one. That is the crux of Canberra's challenge: not simply adjusting to a new order, but navigating a series of transitions, each more demanding than the last.

One likely response from Hugh is that Australia should pursue self-reliance regardless of how the system evolves. Whatever structure emerges, we must, in his view, be able to defend ourselves without relying on great and powerful friends. That principle is clear and consistent. But in a region where multiple great powers are rising – some nuclear-armed, others just large and unpredictable – the meaning of self-reliance becomes more contested, and its realisation more difficult.

What does it mean to be self-reliant, for instance, if China poses a high-end military threat, India challenges us in the Indian Ocean, and a conventionally powerful Indonesia begins exerting pressure in our own neighbourhood? Are we preparing for one adversary, or several? Are we defending the continent, our lines of supply, or a regional order? And how do we avoid the trap of arming for the wrong threat at the wrong time? In a bipolar world, the direction of danger is clearer. In a multipolar one, it multiplies. A force posture calibrated to resist nuclear coercion from China could prove irrelevant in the face of conventional conflict with a great-power Indonesia. Strategic weight still matters and even an Australia that spends much more on defence will never match the scale of several simultaneous great-power challengers. In a world of many giants, agility may prove more important than autonomy.

That insight echoes Hedley Bull's: that Australia must think for itself – and think ahead – in a region where the balance of power is constantly shifting. Bull warned of the dangers of lagging behind. Hugh has warned of the dangers of depending too much for too long. My warning is that the region ahead will be harder and more demanding than even Hugh, in his pessimism, anticipates. And our greatest challenge will not be self-reliance but strategic agility: the ability to move with the region as it changes and to know when the future has already arrived.

Brendan Taylor

HARD NEW WORLD

Correspondence

Clive Edwards

Hugh White's main message is that the world is moving to a multipolar order, from one where America has been the dominant power, especially since the dissolution of the Soviet Union in 1991, to one where at least five powers – America, China, Western Europe, Russia and India – share global leadership, each with its own sphere of influence.

"China's aim," White says, "is clear. Like Russia, it wants to take its place alongside America in the top tier of a multipolar order. To do that it must push America out of East Asia and the Western Pacific." By posing the challenge this way, further discussion is inevitably locked into the near term and the focus is on how America is likely to respond and on "flashpoints … where the rubber meets the road," such as Taiwan.

If, instead, we switch attention to what would seem to be another Chinese aim, industrial development, we get a different global power outcome, one where India is not as influential as White suggests, and which presents a longer-term perspective for defence planning, and for Australian companies too.

As we look at China, it would seem fair to argue that it is in the early years of a significant industrial revolution. In some respects, China resembles America in 1900, when industrialisation took off there on the bases of scale production, technological and product innovation and mass marketing. The difference is that China has relied far more heavily on the world market than did America. Making your way in the world market is not easy, but China has been a high achiever.

Consider solar panels. No other country in the world would be capable of producing this product on the massive scale China currently produces them. It is the most cost-competitive location for the manufacture of all the components in the photovoltaic supply chain. Not only are the panels cheap because of scale production, but they are constantly being upgraded to incorporate technological advances. They are sold around the world. Australia has been a beneficiary. We could produce them ourselves, but not on a scale and at a unit cost that could compare with China's and we would not get the feedback from consumers around the world that Chinese producers get, which stimulates innovation and technological advance.

The solar panel story is not an isolated one. It is being repeated in electric cars, high-speed trains, semiconductors, batteries (for solar power systems, cars) and many other products.

While China has a large domestic market that will contribute far more to demand in the future, Chinese firms and the government are aware of the benefits gained from global involvement and are determined to continue to seek them. Such involvement has been a significant element in the remarkable success of Japan since the 1960s and of South Korea and Taiwan from the 1970s. China observed their experience and has used similar development approaches in many key industries (steel, shipbuilding, motor vehicles, semiconductors). We are today familiar with many Japanese and South Korean brands: Toyota, Honda, Samsung, Hyundai. We are right now getting to know Chinese brands such as BYD, Chery, Great Wall Motors (GWM), Tencent, Haier and Huawei.

In his vision of a multipolar world, White sees India as an important balancing power to the emergence of Chinese hegemony in the Indo-Pacific and Eurasia. The contrast between China's industrial development trajectory and that of India could not be starker. India's development is based principally on its huge home market. Few Indian firms are as globally involved as are many Chinese firms. While we are very aware of Chinese products in Australia, we hardly see any Indian products and we would struggle to name an Indian brand.

What does this difference in development emphasis mean?

China is set to continue its current development trajectory in the decades ahead. In a recent phone conversation between China's president, Xi Jinping, and South Korea's newly elected president, Lee Jae-myung, Xi discussed at length the need for cooperation between the two countries to safeguard multilateralism and free trade. Admittedly this was after Trump's "Liberation Day" tariff onslaught, but it nevertheless underscores how central global participation is to China.

All the East Asian countries are benefiting from China's industrialisation. Trade, investment, technology and research links are significant, have grown over the past thirty and more years and will increase in the future. Singapore and Malaysia, for example, are planning the development of a massive industrial estate the size of Singapore itself in southern Johor. Why? Because they are aware that there will be a movement of industrial capacity within this whole developing East Asian region over the next decades and they seek to participate.

Another point deserves emphasis. All the East Asian countries are development-oriented and are successfully penetrating global markets with their products. Just fifty years ago, tourism was a major Thai industry. Today, Thailand is an important assembler of motor vehicles, most destined for the world market, not the home market. Vietnam's development over the past thirty years has likewise been dramatic, based on supplying manufactured products to world markets.

Now consider India. There is no comparable interconnectedness between India and its neighbours. Sri Lanka is at a vastly different level of development today from Taiwan and yet it is as close geographically to India as Taiwan is to China. It is proximate to Tamil-dominated southern India, one of the most dynamic, business-oriented regions in India, and yet Sri Lanka has stagnated for the past fifty and more years. Pakistan, Afghanistan, Myanmar and Bhutan are all struggling economies. None gets much development impetus from its proximity to India. Manufacturing is small-scale and home-market-oriented. The global footprint of their firms is negligible. The same is true of the land-locked 'stans' (Kazakhstan, Kyrgyzstan, Tajikistan, Turkmenistan and Uzbekistan).

As we look to the future, China's sphere of influence is set to become more and more economically powerful. Japan, South Korea, Taiwan and all the Southeast Asian countries (with a few exceptions like Myanmar) will likely increase their business and other forms of interdependence with China and each other. India, on the other hand, will struggle to develop a sphere of influence based on the glue that, at base level, holds spheres together, dynamic business connections. Even in Eurasia, India will face growing competition for influence, particularly from China but also from Russia. The sheer attractiveness of doing business in East Asia in the future may well suck Indian business interests into China's orbit.

Whichever way one looks at it, the next thirty years could well see China and the countries in its sphere of interest focus on building wealth, thereby delivering another lengthy period when Australia faces a relatively benign Indo-Pacific region. Australia certainly ought to promote trade, investment and other relations with India, but the breadth, depth and growth rate of opportunities in East Asia in the future are likely to be quite breathtaking. It is reasonably obvious where Australia's real interest lies. Australia is in the incredibly fortunate position of proximity to what has been and will likely continue to be a highly innovative, high-growth region of the world.

One further point. Taiwan has become a stumbling block for Australia. We need to see its future in perspective. It has a population of 23 million. Like China, Japan and South Korea, fertility is below replacement and has been for some time, so its population is ageing rapidly and will decline to around 15 million by 2070. It has major links (trade, investment, research) with neighbouring Chinese provinces (Fujian, Jiangxi, Zhejiang, Guangdong). Globally, semiconductor production has been a leading industry over the last thirty years. Trump is currently pressuring its key firm, TSMC, to switch its productive capacity and highly innovative research activities to America. If he is successful, that would represent a major blow to Taiwan. Like that of other Northeast Asian countries, Taiwan's education system places emphasis on STEM subjects. Now and in the years ahead, more and more graduates will find careers in those neighbouring Chinese provinces, which are themselves developing Silicon Valley–type research centres.

Taiwan in the future will be more integrated with and dependent on China than it is today, and the degree of dependence today is high. China would be aware that a summary move on Taiwan would cast a shadow over what would seem to be a key priority in the coming decades: solidifying its sphere of influence. As White says, it will likely tread carefully. And Australia and America need to appreciate that Taiwan has no viable future if its links with China are severed. Should that happen, the majority of Taiwan's population would have to migrate elsewhere. Most would go to China. Would Australia really join America in a war with China over Taiwan, which could turn nuclear, where the outcome would be an island cut off from the mainland with a very much smaller, poorer population that would have no alternative but to return progressively to the previous status quo of interdependence with the mainland, political this time as well as economic? White is right when he says, "We should tell Washington that we will not go to war over Taiwan," but we should clearly explain our reasoning.

White concludes that our focus "must be to help create a new order in Asia." China and the East Asian region together are doing that. We just need to fit in. The new world order may be hard for European countries, but it is not significantly harder for Australia. It is one of opportunity. Australia's strategic circumstances are no more threatening today than they have been at any time since World War II.

Clive Edwards

Response to Correspondence

Hugh White

It is fair to say, I think, that all of the eight distinguished commentators who have been kind enough to offer these responses to *Hard New World* agree with what is, I suppose, its underlying premise: that Australia today faces significant changes in its strategic circumstances as the distribution of power and resolve shifts among this region's stronger powers, leaving America relatively weaker, less influential and less useful to Australia than we have long assumed. And while I learnt long ago that there is no dignified nor useful way to say "I told you so," I am grateful to many of them for generously acknowledging that I have been arguing for this now widely accepted proposition for fifteen years or more.

But it is old news. What is new is how fast these changes are happening, and how far they are going. That is the key focus of *Hard New World*. I have tried to show that America's post–Cold War role globally and in key regions is collapsing more quickly and more completely than has generally been recognised, thanks to the failures of the Biden administration, the trajectory of the Russia–Ukraine War, and the spectacle of Donald Trump's second administration.

I have also tried to offer a deeper explanation of this collapse, based on the changing balance between the imperatives for America to exercise global strategic leadership and the costs of doing so. On the one hand, I suggest that with the return in this century of something like the nineteenth century's genuinely multipolar global distribution of wealth and power, America need no longer fear, as it did for so much of the twentieth century, the emergence of a Eurasian hegemon which might threaten America itself. On the other hand, the emergence of several peer competitors raises the costs to America of exercising global hegemony far beyond what the architects and visionaries of a post–Cold War US-led world order imagined. That is why it makes sense for America to step back from major strategic commitments beyond the Western Hemisphere, as it did in the nineteenth century.

I'll confess to being a little surprised, and perhaps a little disappointed, that none of these responses to the essay have addressed or contested this key argument, because if it is right – and I am pretty sure it is – the implications for the future of the global order, for the strategic balance in Asia and for our alliance with America are profound. Moreover, I am struck by the fact that while they agree that America's role is waning, most of the respondents suggest America will remain a big influence on Australia's strategic environment, and an important strategic asset for Australia, for a long time to come. Accordingly, they are, I think, more relaxed and comfortable than I am about the need to swiftly reframe our foreign and defence policies.

Let me start with my dear old friend and colleague Brendan Taylor, from whom I have learnt so much over the years. He argues elegantly that I exaggerate the significance and difficulty of the transition now underway in the Asian strategic order, for two reasons. First, he sees this shift as just one of a long series of transformations in the Asian order to which Australia has adapted in the past and will have to keep adapting to in future. Second, he thinks America will continue to retain significant roles in the succession of regional orders he expects over the decades ahead, making those adaptations easier for Australia than I suggest.

Taylor is quite right to say that the regional order will keep changing and Australia will have to keep adapting to those changes, and it is an important insight. But I do not think he is right to see the current transition as just one in a long series, no more significant than many we have encountered and managed before. That is because the era of US-led unipolarity in East Asia and the Western Pacific that is now passing away goes back much further than he seems to think. America has been the primary maritime power in this region almost continually since the end of the nineteenth century. Its place was only challenged once, by imperial Japan, and that challenge was swiftly and decisively crushed. The Soviet Union was never a significant strategic rival to America in East Asia, and after Mao's accommodation with Washington in 1972 America's regional primacy was essentially uncontested – until China's current challenge began around 2010. Like Taylor, I have long been a fan of Hedley Bull's 1974 essay on the great powers in Asia. But it turns out Hedley was wrong about what was happening to the regional order at that time. There was no shift to a quadripolar power structure involving America, the Soviet Union, China and Japan. What we saw instead was sustained, and indeed strengthened, US unipolarity.

It having lasted so long, that the regional order based on American primacy should be ending is thus a very big deal indeed. It is an especially big deal for Australia, which more than any other country in the region has depended on America to define our place in Asia. And it is an even bigger deal when we remember that before America we relied in the same way on Britain, all the way back to 1788. That is why, as I argue, we have never been through a transformation like this before; the eclipse of US power in Asia is the biggest shift in Australia's international setting since European settlement. And we haven't begun seriously to respond to that.

That brings me to the second reason Taylor has for being more relaxed about our predicament than I am. He thinks America will remain a key strategic power in Asia, constituting one of the great-power poles in each of the succession of changing polarities. That is because, he says, it still has "unmatched power projection capabilities and a sprawling network of regional allies and partners." As I argue at length in my essay, I think this simply fails to see how much things have already changed and how strongly the big global shifts are undermining the US position. Those who think America will retain a significant strategic role in Asia need to explain how and why it will do that in the very different circumstances of the decades ahead.

James Curran, too, is more optimistic than I am about America's future in Asia. He mentions, reasonably enough, the mixed messages in the Trump administration's approach to the strategic challenge from China, citing Defense Secretary Hegseth's hawkish speech in Singapore in June 2025. I think Trump's own views are clear, and will prevail. But more importantly, neither Trump's views nor Hegseth's nor anyone else's matter much to the big question if I am right about the deeper forces pulling America back from its long strategic engagement in Asia and Europe.

Ali Wyne, one of America's most nuanced thinkers about his country's future in Asia, is also confident that America can and will remain a key player in the region. He says it is premature to predict US withdrawal when one considers the deepening of US "military and technological relationships with countries including Australia, India, Japan, the Philippines and Vietnam." But as I argue in the essay, it is precisely the feebleness of these measures, and their clear inadequacy to redress the massive shift in military advantage from America to China over recent decades, that demonstrates how successive administrations in Washington have in effect begun America's withdrawal from Asia by failing to meet China's challenge.

Wyne has much of interest to say about the uncertain trajectory of the second Trump administration's China policy, as the contest plays out between the MAGA movement's isolationism and the Washington establishment's residual attachment to US global leadership. But, like Curran, he seems to attach more importance to these debates than they deserve. America's future in Asia will ultimately be determined not by the ebb and flow of beltway debates but by the lack of a compelling strategic reason for America to shoulder the massive costs and risks of preserving a strong US strategic role in Asia in the face of China's determination that it should leave the region.

This is not to deny the importance of Trump and his movement to our assessment of America's future in Asia. Indeed, one of the core messages of *Hard New World* is that Trump's second term as US president shows that American politics and government have changed in some fundamental way which makes it impossible for us to expect that the old Washington, with its cosy bipartisanship in support of a traditional model of US global leadership, will ever return. This seems to be overlooked by those who remain confident that America will retain a key strategic role in Asia, because that presupposes US politics can rebuild a durable and workable consensus around that role. There is no sign of that.

Emma Shortis, in her thoughtful commentary, clearly understands this, and so she sees more realistically how little we can look to America to support Asian order or Australia's future security. I would simply note, though, that while we should not underestimate Trump's importance, nor should we overestimate it. He is not a temporary aberration that will soon pass, allowing America to return to normal, but America's withdrawal from global leadership is not all down to Trump. That would be happening whoever was in the White House, because of the fundamental realities of global power I have mentioned.

One of those realities that seems to me especially important is the reappearance, after a thirty-five-year hiatus, of nuclear weapons as a decisive factor in great-power politics. I believe this has been decisively demonstrated by the way Russia's invasion of Ukraine has played out, which is why I explored it at some length in the essay. I am especially grateful to Mark Edele, a noted authority in this field, for his very interesting comments on my analysis. He knows a lot more about Russia and Ukraine than I do, but there are a couple of points about the strategic dynamics of this tragedy on which I'd like to test his judgements.

One is the question of whether Russia is a great power. Edele says it isn't. I think that on balance it is, despite its relative weakness in many of the dimensions of national power. Much depends, of course, on how one defines "great power." My definition is that a country is a great power when it has the power to defy and disrupt an international order which does not respect its vital interests, and whose interests must therefore be – at least to some extent – accommodated if the international order is to be made viable. On this definition I think Russia is in the process of demonstrating in Ukraine that it is, once again, a great power. It is doing that by forcing the rest of us, and America and Europe especially, to accept its claims to exert a degree of hegemonic influence over Ukraine that is incompatible with the old "rules-based order" of the post–Cold War era. The fact that those claims are now accepted is clear from the terms, once categorically rejected, which now seem to be acknowledged by Ukraine and its supporters as the basis for an end to the war. They include Russia's retention of significant Ukrainian territory and the abandonment of Ukraine's ambitions to join NATO. How has Russia done this, given its weakness relative to Ukraine's supporters in America and Europe? I argue that the answer is its nuclear weapons.

Edele downplays the significance of Russia's nuclear weapons because he does not think Moscow's threats to use them have been credible. I acknowledge that his view is shared by many other noted commentators, but it does not seem to have been shared by the people whose opinion really matters: national leaders in Washington and the capitals of Europe. I think they have been right about that. It is true that, as Edele says, Putin has never made good on his nuclear threats. But that is because, as he also says, Russia has never faced a devastating defeat in its war with Ukraine. Had it done so, the risk that it would use nuclear weapons in the absence of any credible threat of nuclear retaliation is very real: real enough to deter Western powers from providing Kyiv the support required to inflict such a defeat. Hence my conclusion that, in today's world, nuclear weapons can endow even relatively weak powers with the strategic weight of a great power. And in case this is not crystal clear, my bleak conclusion is not in any way an endorsement of Russia's conduct or a condemnation of Ukraine's. It is simply an attempt realistically to describe the realities of the hard new world we have to deal with.

Russia is not the only country with questionable claims to being a great power in the new multipolar global order. Clive Edwards makes some excellent points about India's shortcomings. Many people in Canberra, Washington and elsewhere have been keen to talk up India's potential to match and overtake Chinese power, arguing that it can thereby help counterbalance China's influence and help sustain the US-led order. But Edwards argues that India's economic trajectory is, so far at least, very different from China's, and that there are far fewer opportunities for Delhi to build regional sway comparable to China's. I think this is right, though I would add a note of caution. India's economic rise – and Indonesia's – is not following the now familiar East Asian pattern, nor does it match its extraordinary speed. But that does not mean these nations cannot find their own way to economic development, slower perhaps and more erratic than their East Asian neighbours but delivering enough wealth and power for them to function as great powers. And even if its GDP remains far behind China's, India will wield considerable and increasing strategic weight – including nuclear weapons. So India's economic shortcomings compared to China will not prevent it from playing a decisive strategic role in South Asia and the northern Indian Ocean, and from resisting any Chinese effort to assert hegemony over that region. Thus it will not preclude the emergence of the multipolar Asia divided between Chinese and Indian spheres of influence, with no significant US presence, that I sketch in the essay.

The question remains how Australia should best prepare to make its way in this very different Asia. Susannah Patton suggests we are already doing enough. She thinks we have been doing a fine job of deepening our relations with key regional countries, including India, Japan and Indonesia, pointing to new declarations, meetings, agreements and exercises that have been initiated in recent years. More broadly, she takes me to task for, she says, reviving the old argument that we need to distance ourselves from America in order to build "true engagement" with the countries of our region.

Let me deal with that issue first. There has for a long time been a progressive, essentially anti-American view that our US alliance posed an insuperable barrier to effective relations in the region. That was plainly wrong while America's role as the region's leading power was essentially uncontested, as it was from the early 1970s until fifteen years ago. Over those happy decades both America's and Australia's vision of regional order was essentially identical to that of our neighbours'. But that is no longer the situation today. As China's challenge to US leadership in Asia has intensified, a wide gap has opened between the US and Australian vision of regional order and our Southeast Asian neighbours' vision. We have sided unambiguously with Washington – the old pre-Trump Washington. Notwithstanding Penny Wong's occasional invocation of "balance," we have stuck to the view that continued US leadership is the only possible foundation for regional order. Moreover, we have accepted that, if necessary, we are willing to go to war with China to uphold that vision, because that is what AUKUS and all the talk of "deterrence" means – if it means anything. Our neighbours have very pointedly taken a different path. They have refused to take sides between Washington and Bejing, and they certainly reject any idea of going to war with China to support America. I do not think we can work effectively with our Southeast Asian neighbours to help shape the future regional order unless this yawning gap between our visions of that order is closed. And because I think their vision makes more sense than ours, for all the reasons set out in the essay, it is we who should change.

Which brings us back to the effectiveness of our recent regional diplomacy. What is striking about Patton's catalogue of recent advances in strategic and defence relations with India, Japan and other regional countries is that they are all intended – on our side at least – to foster the impression, or one might say the illusion, of a united coalition in support of America against China. As long as that is the focus of our regional diplomacy, we will get nowhere in developing the relations we need to make our way in the hard new region we are going to confront in the decades ahead, rather than the one we might wish to see.

Of course, this is all very scary stuff, and no one should be surprised that our political leaders, our public servants and many of our commentators shy away from confronting it. But with these great challenges come great opportunities – especially for political leaders. In the last few weeks we have seen Prime Minister Albanese invoke the bold and courageous statesmanship with which John Curtin, with his turn to America, and Gough Whitlam, with his opening to China, confronted comparably critical moments in our history. Is it possible that he does not see how far he is from following their example, and earning a comparable place in history, in his timid response to today's challenges? Might he be persuaded to abandon his timidity and emulate his Labor heroes?

Lachlan Harris, in his wise and intriguing comment on the essay, is so right to step back from the strategic arguments and explore the wider political and national issues at stake in the way we address them. Whether we can redefine ourselves as a country and reframe the way we make our way in the very different post-American world of the twenty-first century is a question that goes far beyond the specific issues involved. It goes to the heart of our politics and our national life. Harris's bracingly optimistic conclusion is that if we can get this right – and I think we can – then it offers a springboard to get a lot of other things right for our country too. All I can say in response is, "Yes, I agree."

Hugh White

James Curran is a professor of modern history at the University of Sydney and a foreign affairs columnist with *The Australian Financial Review.*

Mark Edele is Hansen Professor in History at the University of Melbourne. His latest book is *Russia's War Against Ukraine: The Whole Story* (second edition forthcoming).

Clive Edwards is an academic economist (ANU, University of Queensland). The focus of his research has been on the different strategies used by the East Asian countries to achieve quite stunning success since the 1960s.

Lachlan Harris is an entrepreneur and served as principal press secretary to Prime Minister Kevin Rudd.

Susannah Patton is deputy research director of the Lowy Institute, and the director of the Southeast Asia Program, responsible for the Asia Power Index.

Emma Shortis is director of the international and security affairs program at the Australia Institute.

Brendan Taylor is a professor of strategic studies and head of the Strategic and Defence Studies Centre at the Australian National University.

Hugh White is the author of *The China Choice* and *How to Defend Australia*, and four acclaimed Quarterly Essays. He is emeritus professor of strategic studies at the Australian National University and was the principal author of Australia's Defence White Paper 2000.

Marian Wilkinson is a multi-award-winning investigative journalist and former reporter at ABC TV's *Four Corners*. She has been a foreign correspondent and deputy editor for *The Sydney Morning Herald* and an executive producer of *Four Corners*. Her books include *The Fixer*, *Dark Victory* (with David Marr) and *The Carbon Club*.

Ali Wyne is the senior research and advocacy adviser for US–China relations at the International Crisis Group.

QUARTERLY ESSAY BACK ISSUES

- ☐ **QE 1** *In Denial* by Robert Manne $27.99
- ☐ **QE 2** *Appeasing Jakarta* by John Birmingham $27.99
- ☐ **QE 3** *The Opportunist* by Guy Rundle $27.99
- ☐ **QE 4** *Rabbit Syndrome* by Don Watson $27.99
- ☐ **QE 5** *Girt By Sea* by Mungo MacCallum $27.99
- ☐ **QE 6** *Beyond Belief* by John Button $27.99
- ☐ **QE 7** *Paradise Betrayed* by John Martinkus $27.99
- **QE 8** *Groundswell* by Amanda Lohrey OUT OF STOCK
- ☐ **QE 9** *Beautiful Lies* by Tim Flannery $27.99
- ☐ **QE 10** *Bad Company* by Gideon Haigh $27.99
- ☐ **QE 11** *Whitefella Jump Up* by Germaine Greer $27.99
- ☐ **QE 12** *Made in England* by David Malouf $27.99
- ☐ **QE 13** *Sending Them Home* by Robert Manne with David Corlett $27.99
- ☐ **QE 14** *Mission Impossible* by Paul McGeough $27.99
- ☐ **QE 15** *Latham's World* by Margaret Simons $27.99
- ☐ **QE 16** *Breach of Trust* by Raimond Gaita $27.99
- ☐ **QE 17** *'Kangaroo Court'* by John Hirst $27.99
- ☐ **QE 18** *The Worried Well* by Gail Bell $27.99
- ☐ **QE 19** *Relaxed & Comfortable* by Judith Brett $27.99
- ☐ **QE 20** *A Time for War* by John Birmingham $27.99
- ☐ **QE 21** *What's Left? by Clive Hamilton* $27.99
- ☐ **QE 22** *Voting for Jesus* by Amanda Lohrey $27.99
- ☐ **QE 23** *The History Question* by Inga Clendinnen $27.99
- ☐ **QE 24** *No Fixed Address* by Robyn Davidson $27.99
- ☐ **QE 25** *Bipolar Nation* by Peter Hartcher $27.99
- ☐ **QE 26** *His Master's Voice* by David Marr $27.99
- ☐ **QE 27** *Reaction Time* by Ian Lowe $27.99
- ☐ **QE 28** *Exit Right* by Judith Brett $27.99
- ☐ **QE 29** *Love & Money* by Anne Manne $27.99
- ☐ **QE 30** *Last Drinks* by Paul Toohey $27.99
- ☐ **QE 31** *Now or Never* by Tim Flannery $27.99
- ☐ **QE 32** *American Revolution* by Kate Jennings $27.99
- ☐ **QE 33** *Quarry Vision* by Guy Pearse $27.99
- ☐ **QE 34** *Stop at Nothing* by Annabel Crabb $27.99
- ☐ **QE 35** *Radical Hope* by Noel Pearson $27.99
- ☐ **QE 36** *Australian Story* by Mungo MacCallum $27.99
- ☐ **QE 37** *What's Right?* by Waleed Aly $27.99
- ☐ **QE 38** *Power Trip* by David Marr $27.99
- ☐ **QE 39** *Power Shift* by Hugh White $27.99
- ☐ **QE 40** *Trivial Pursuit* by George Megalogenis $27.99
- ☐ **QE 41** *The Happy Life* by David Malouf $27.99
- ☐ **QE 42** *Fair Share* by Judith Brett $27.99
- ☐ **QE 43** *Bad News* by Robert Manne $27.99
- ☐ **QE 44** *Man-Made World* by Andrew Charlton $27.99
- ☐ **QE 45** *Us and Them* by Anna Krien $27.99
- ☐ **QE 46** *Great Expectations* by Laura Tingle $27.99
- ☐ **QE 47** *Political Animal* by David Marr $27.99
- ☐ **QE 48** *After the Future* by Tim Flannery $27.99
- ☐ **QE 49** *Not Dead Yet* by Mark Latham $27.99
- ☐ **QE 50** *Unfinished Business* by Anna Goldsworthy $27.99
- ☐ **QE 51** *The Prince* by David Marr $27.99
- ☐ **QE 52** *Found in Translation* by Linda Jaivin $27.99
- ☐ **QE 53** *That Sinking Feeling* by Paul Toohey $27.99
- ☐ **QE 54** *Dragon's Tail* by Andrew Charlton $27.99
- ☐ **QE 55** *A Rightful Place* by Noel Pearson $27.99
- ☐ **QE 56** *Clivosaurus* by Guy Rundle $27.99
- ☐ **QE 57** *Dear Life* by Karen Hitchcock $27.99
- ☐ **QE 58** *Blood Year* by David Kilcullen $27.99
- ☐ **QE 59** *Faction Man* by David Marr $27.99
- ☐ **QE 60** *Political Amnesia* by Laura Tingle $27.99
- ☐ **QE 61** *Balancing Act* by George Megalogenis $27.99
- ☐ **QE 62** *Firing Line* by James Brown $27.99
- ☐ **QE 63** *Enemy Within* by Don Watson $27.99
- ☐ **QE 64** *The Australian Dream* by Stan Grant $27.99
- ☐ **QE 65** *The White Queen* by David Marr $27.99
- ☐ **QE 66** *The Long Goodbye* by Anna Krien $27.99
- ☐ **QE 67** *Moral Panic 101* by Benjamin Law $27.99
- ☐ **QE 68** *Without America* by Hugh White $27.99

QUARTERLY ESSAY BACK ISSUES

- ☐ **QE 69** *Moment of Truth* by Mark McKenna $27.99
- ☐ **QE 70** *Dead Right* by Richard Denniss $27.99
- ☐ **QE 71** *Follow the Leader* by Laura Tingle $27.99
- ☐ **QE 72** *Net Loss* by Sebastian Smee $27.99
- ☐ **QE 73** *Australia Fair* by Rebecca Huntley $27.99
- ☐ **QE 74** *The Prosperity Gospel* by Erik Jensen $27.99
- ☐ **QE 75** *Men at Work* by Annabel Crabb $27.99
- ☐ **QE 76** *Red Flag* by Peter Hartcher $27.99
- ☐ **QE 77** *Cry Me a River* by Margaret Simons $27.99
- ☐ **QE 78** *The Coal Curse* by Judith Brett $27.99
- ☐ **QE 79** *The End of Certainty* by Katharine Murphy $27.99
- ☐ **QE 80** *The High Road* by Laura Tingle $27.99
- ☐ **QE 81** *Getting to Zero* by Alan Finkel $27.99
- ☐ **QE 82** *Exit Strategy* by George Megalogenis $27.99
- ☐ **QE 83** *Top Blokes* by Lech Blaine $27.99
- ☐ **QE 84** *The Reckoning* by Jess Hill $27.99
- ☐ **QE 85** *Not Waving, Drowning* by Sarah Krasnostein $27.99
- ☐ **QE 86** *Sleepwalk to War* by Hugh White $27.99
- ☐ **QE 87** *Uncivil Wars* by Waleed Aly & Scott Stephens $27.99
- ☐ **QE 88** *Lone Wolf* by Katharine Murphy $27.99
- ☐ **QE 89** *The Wires That Bind* by Saul Griffith $27.99
- ☐ **QE 90** *Voice of Reason* by Megan Davis $27.99
- ☐ **QE 91** *Lifeboat* by Micheline Lee $27.99
- ☐ **QE 92** *The Great Divide* by Alan Kohler $27.99
- ☐ **QE 93** *Bad Cop* by Lech Blaine $27.99
- ☐ **QE 94** *Highway to Hell* by Joëlle Gergis $27.99
- ☐ **QE 95** *High Noon* by Don Watson $27.99
- ☐ **QE 96** *Minority Report* by George Megalogenis $29.99
- ☐ **QE 97** *Losing It* by Jess Hill $29.99
- ☐ **QE 98** *Hard New World* by Hugh White $29.99

Order back issues online

Prices include GST.
$10 flat-rate shipping within Australia.
Please include this form with delivery and payment details overleaf.
Back issues also available as ebooks from ebook retailers.

SUBSCRIBE TO SAVE NEARLY $20 OFF THE COVER PRICE

☐ **ONE-YEAR PRINT AND DIGITAL SUBSCRIPTION: $99.99**

- Print edition
- Home delivery
- Automatically renewing
- Full digital access to all past issues
- App for Android and iPhone users
- ebook files

DELIVERY AND PAYMENT DETAILS

DELIVERY DETAILS:

NAME:

ADDRESS:

EMAIL: PHONE:

PAYMENT DETAILS: Enclose a cheque/money order made out to Schwartz Books Pty Ltd.
Or debit my credit card (MasterCard, Visa and Amex accepted).
Freepost: Quarterly Essay, Reply Paid 90094, Collingwood VIC 3066
All prices include GST, postage and handling.

CARD NO.

EXPIRY DATE: / CCV: AMOUNT: $

PURCHASER'S NAME: SIGNATURE:

Subscribe online at **quarterlyessay.com/subscribe** • Freecall: 1800 077 514 • Phone: 03 9486 0288
Email: subscribe@quarterlyessay.com (please do not send electronic scans of this form)